FLAT STANLEY

Stanley's Christmas Adventure

by Jeff Brown
Pictures by Macky Pamintuan

FOR DUNCAN

Stanley's Christmas Adventure

Text copyright © 1993 by Jeff Brown
Illustrations by Macky Pamintuan, copyright © 2010 by HarperCollins Publishers
All rights reserved.

Published in agreement with the author, c/o BAROR INTERNATIONAL, INC., Armonk, New York, U.S.A. through Danny Hong Agency, Seoul, Korea.

ISBN 979-11-91343-67-0 14740

Longtail Books

CONTENTS

Prologue

She was the sort of little girl who liked to be *sure* of things, so she went all over Snow City, **check**ing **up**.

The elves* had done their work.

At the Post Office, Mail Elves had read

★ **elf** 미국, 캐나다, 영국의 민간전승에서 산타클로스의 조수로 등장하는 아주 작은 요정. 북극에 있는 공장에서 크리스마스 선물인 장난감을 생산하고 포장한다.

5

the letters, making lists of who wanted what.

In the great **workshop**s—the Doll Room, the Toy **Plant**, the Game **Mill**— Gift Elves had **fill**ed the orders, **taking care** as to color and size and style.

In the **Wrap Shed** the gifts lay ready, wrapped now in **gay** paper with holly* and **pine cone**s, sorted by country, by city or village, by road or **lane** or street.

The Wrap Elves **tease**d her. "Don't trust

us, eh? . . . **Snoop**ing, we call this, Miss!"

"Pooh!" said the little girl. "Well done, elves! Good work!"

But at home in Snow City **Square**, all was not well.

"Don't **slam** the door, **dear**," said her mother, **weep**ing. "Your father's having his **nap**."

"Mother! What's wrong?"

"He won't go this year, he says!" The mother **sob**bed. "He's been so **cross lately**, but I never—"

"*Why? Why* won't he go?"

"They've lost **faith**, don't care anymore,

★**holly** 호랑가시나무. 잎가에 뾰족뾰족한 가시가 돋아 있고 새빨간 열매가 달리는 나무로 흔히 크리스마스 장식으로 쓰인다.

he says! Surely not *everyone*, I said. Think of your favorite letter, the one by your desk! He just **growl**ed at me!"

"Pooh!" said the girl. "It's not fair! Really! I mean, everything's *ready!* Why—"

"Not now, dear," said the mother. "It's been a **dreadful** day."

In the little office at the back of the house, the girl studied the letter her mother had **mention**ed, **frame**d with others on a wall:

I am a regular boy, **except** that I got flat, the letter said. From an accident. I was going to ask for new clothes, but my mother already bought them. She had to, because of the flatness. So I'm just writing to say don't **bother** about me.

Have a nice **holiday**. My father says be careful driving, there are lots of bad drivers this time of year.

The girl thought for a moment, and an idea came to her. "Hmmmm . . . Well, why *not?*" she said.

She looked again at the letter.

The name LAMBCHOP was **print**ed across the top, and an **address**. It was **sign**ed "Stanley, U.S.A."

Sarah

It was two nights before Christmas, and all through the house not a Lambchop was **stir**ring, but something was.

Stanley Lambchop sat up in his bed. "Listen! Someone said 'Rat.'"

"It was more like 'grat,'" said his younger brother, Arthur, from his bed. "In the living room, I think."

The brothers **tiptoe**d down the stairs.

For a moment all was silence in the
darkened living room. Then came a *thump*.
"**Ouch!**" said a small voice. "Drat* again!"

"Are you a **burglar**?" Arthur called.
"Did you hurt yourself?"

"I am *not* a burglar!" said the voice.
"Where's the—Ah!" The lights came on.

The brothers **stare**d.

Before the **fireplace**, by the Christmas
tree, stood a **slender**, dark-haired little
girl wearing a red jacket and skirt, both
trimmed with white **fur**.

"I **bang**ed it *twice*," she said, **rub**bing
her **knee**. "Coming down the **chimney**,

★ drat 제기랄! 젠장!

and just now."

"We *do* have a **front door**, you know,"
said Stanley.

"Well, so does my house. But, you know,

this time of year . . . ?" The girl sounded a bit nervous. "Actually, I've never done this before. Let's see . . . Ha, ha, ha! Season's **Greeting**s! Ha, ha, ha!"

"'Ha, ha!' to you," said Arthur. "What's so funny?"

"Funny?" said the girl. "Oh! 'Ho, ho, ho!' I meant. I'm Sarah Christmas. Who are you?"

"Arthur Lambchop," said Arthur. "That's my brother, Stanley."

"It is? But he's not *flat*."

"He was, but I blew him up," Arthur explained. "With a bicycle **pump**."

"Oh, no! I wish you hadn't." Sarah Christmas **sank** into a chair. "Drat! It's all going wrong! Perhaps I shouldn't have come. But that's how I am. **Headstrong**, my mother says. She—"

"Excuse me," Stanley said. "But where are you from?"

"And why *did* you come?" said Arthur. Sarah told them.

Mr. and Mrs. Lambchop were reading in bed.

A **tap** came at the door, and then Stanley's voice. "Hey! Can I come in?"

Mr. and Mrs. Lambchop cared greatly for **proper** speech. "**Hay** is for horses, Stanley," she said. "And not 'can,' **dear**. You *may* come in."

Stanley came in.

"What is the **explanation**, my boy,

of this late **call**?" said Mr. Lambchop,
remembering past surprises. "You have
not, I see, become flat again. Has a genie*
come to visit? Or perhaps the **President** of
the United States has called?"

Mrs. Lambchop smiled. "You are very
amusing, George."

"Arthur and I were in bed," said Stanley.
"But we heard a noise and went to see. It
was a girl called Sarah Christmas, from
Snow City. She talks a lot. She says her
father says he won't come this year, but
Sarah thinks he might change his mind
if I ask him to. Because I wrote him a
letter once that he liked. She wants me to

★ genie 지니. 아라비아 신화에서 병이나 램프 속에 사는 요정.

17

go with her to Snow City. In her father's **sleigh**. It's at the North **Pole**, I think."

Stanley **caught his breath**. "I said I'd have to ask you first."

"Quite right," said Mrs. Lambchop.

Mr. Lambchop went to the bathroom and drank a glass of water to calm himself.

"Now then, Stanley," he said, returning. "You have greatly **startle**d us. Surely—"

"Put on your **robe**, George," said Mrs. Lambchop. "Let us hear for ourselves what this visitor has to say."

"This is *delicious!*" Sarah Christmas **sip**ped the hot chocolate Mrs. Lambchop had **serve**d them all. "My mother makes it too, with cinnamon* in it. And little cookies with—" Her **glance** had fallen on the **mantelpiece**. "What's *that*, **pin**ned up there?"

"Christmas stockings,*" Stanley said. "The blue one's mine."

★ **cinnamon** 시나몬. 향신료의 하나로 매우 자극적인 독특한 향기가 있다.
⚹ **Christmas stocking** 크리스마스에 아이들이 산타클로스의 선물을 받으려고 밤에 머리맡에 걸어 두는 양말.

"But the other, the great **square** thing?"

"It's a **pillowcase**." Arthur **blush**ed. "My stocking wouldn't do. I have very small feet."

"Pooh!" Sarah laughed. "You wanted **extra** gifts, so—"

"Sarah, dear," Mrs. Lambchop said. "Your father? Has he truly **made up his mind**, you think?"

"Oh, yes!" Sarah **sigh**ed. "But I thought—Stanley being flat, that *really* interested him. I mean, I couldn't be *sure*, but if nobody ever did anything without—"

"You seem a very nice girl, Sarah." Mr. Lambchop gave a little laugh. "But you *have* been **joking** with us, surely? I—"

The phone rang, and he answered it.

"Hello, George," the caller said. "This is your **neighbor**, Frank Smith. I know it's late, but I must **congratulate** you on your Christmas **lawn display**! Best—"

"Lawn?" said Mr. Lambchop. "Display?"

"The sleigh! And those **lifelike** *reindeer*! What makes them move about

like that? Batteries, I suppose?"

"Just a moment, Frank." Mr. Lambchop went to the window and looked out, Mrs. Lambchop beside him.

"My **goodness**!" she said. "One, two, three, four . . . Eight! And such a pretty sleigh!"

Mr. Lambchop returned to the phone. "They *are* lifelike, aren't they? Good-bye. Thank you for calling, Frank."

"See? I'm not a joking kind of person, actually," said Sarah Christmas. "Now! My idea *might* work, even without the flatness. Do let Stanley go!"

"To the North Pole?" said Mrs. Lambchop. "At night? By himself? Good **gracious**, Sarah!"

"It's not fair, asking Stanley, but not me," said Arthur, feeling hurt. "It's always like this! I never—"

"Oh, pooh!" Sarah Christmas smiled. "Actually . . . You could *all* go. It's a very big sleigh."

Mr. and Mrs. Lambchop looked at each other, then at Stanley and Arthur, then at each other again.

"Stanley just might make a difference, George," Mrs. Lambchop said. "And if we can *all* go . . . ?"

"Quite right," said Mr. Lambchop. "Sarah, we will **accompany** you to Snow City!"

"**Hooray**!" shouted Stanley and Arthur, and Sarah too.

Mrs. Lambchop thought they should wait until Frank Smith had gone to bed. "**Imagine** the **gossip**," she said, "were he to see our reindeer fly away."

Mr. Lambchop called his office to leave a message on the **nighttime** answering machine. He would not be in tomorrow, he said, as he had been called **unexpected**ly **out of town**.

"There!" cried Stanley, by the window. "The Smiths' light is out."

The Lambchops changed quickly from **pajamas** to warmer clothing, and followed Sarah to the sleigh.

The Sleigh

"Welcome **aboard**!" said Sarah, from the driver's seat.

The Lambchops, sitting on little **bench**es that made the big **sleigh resemble** a **roof**less bus, could **scarcely contain** their excitement.

The night sky shone bright with stars, and from the windows of nearby houses red and green Christmas lights **twinkle**d over **snowy lawn**s and streets. Before them, the eight **reindeer, fur** shiny in the moonlight, **toss**ed their **antler**ed heads.

"Ready when you are, Sarah," Mr. Lambchop said.

"Good!" Sarah **clear**ed **her throat**. "**Fasten** your seat belts, please! We **are about to depart** for Snow City. My name is Sarah—I guess you know that—and I'll be glad to answer any questions you may have. Please do not move about without **permission** of the Sleigh **Master**—that's me, at least right now—and **obey** whatever **instruct**ions may—"

"Pu-leeese!" said Arthur.

"Oh, all right!" The Lambchops fastened

their seat belts, and Sarah took up the **rein**s. "Ready, One? Ready, Two, Three—"

"Just *numbers?*" cried Mrs. Lambchop. "Why,* we know such lovely reindeer names! Dasher, Dancer, Prancer, Vixen—"

"Comet, Cupid, Donder, Blitzen!" shouted Arthur. "They're from a **poem*** we know!"

"Those *are* good names!" said Sarah. "Ready, One through Eight?"

The reindeer **paw**ed the ground,

jingling their **harness** bells.

"Now!" said Sarah.

The jingling stopped suddenly, and a great silence fell.

Now a silver **mist** rose, **swirl**ing, about the sleigh. The **startle**d Lambchops could

---

★ **why** 여기에서는 '왜'라는 뜻의 의문사가 아니라, '아니!', '어머!'라는 의미의 감탄사로 쓰였다.

✻ **poem** 여기에서 말하는 시는 Clement Clarke Moore가 쓴 "'Twas the Night Before Christmas"이다. 가장 유명한 크리스마스 시 가운데 하나로, 여기에 나오는 여덟 순록의 이름이 바로 Dasher, Dancer, Prancer, Vixen, Comet, Cupid, Donder, 그리고 Blitzen이다. 크리스마스이브에 이 시를 어린아이에게 읽어주는 것이 오랜 전통이다.

see nothing beyond the mist, not their house nor the houses of their **neighbor**s, not the twinkling Christmas lights, not the bright stars above. There was only the silver mist, everywhere, cool against their **cheek**s.

"What is this, Sarah?" Mrs. Lambchop called. "Are we not to **proceed** to Snow City?"

Sarah's voice came **cheerful**ly through the mist. "We have proceeded. We're there!"

Snow City

Beyond the **mist**, excited voices rose.

"Sarah's back! . . . With strangers! Big ones!
. . . Where's she been?"

"Poppa's elves," said Sarah's voice.

As she spoke, the mist **swirl**ed, then
vanished as suddenly as it had come.

Above them, the stars shone bright again.

The sleigh **rest**ed now in a snow-covered

square, in front of a pretty red-**roof**ed house. All about the square were **tiny cottage**s, their windows **aglow** with light.

Elves **surround**ed the sleigh. "Who *are* these people?" . . . "Is it true, what we've heard?" . . . "Ask Sarah! She'll know!"

The Lambchops smiled and **wave**d. The elves seemed much like **ordinary** men and women, **except** that they had **pointy** ears, very **wrinkle**d faces, and were only about half as tall as Arthur. All wore **leather breeches** or skirts with wide pockets from which **tool**s and **needle**s **stuck out**.

"Miss Sarah!" came a voice. "Is it true? He won't go this year?"

Sarah **hesitate**d. "Well, sort of . . . But perhaps the Lambchops here . . . Be

patient. Go home, please!"

The elves **straggle**d off toward their cottages, **grumbling**. "Not going?" . . . "Hah! After all our work?" . . . "The *Who*chops?" . . . "I'd go work somewhere else, but *where?*"

A **plump** lady in an **apron bustle**d out of the red-roofed house. "Sarah! Are you all right? Going off like that! Though we

did find your **note**. **Gracious**! Are those *all*
Lambchops, **dear**?"

"I'm fine, Momma!" said Sarah. "They
wouldn't let Stanley come by himself.
That's Stanley, there. The other one's
Arthur. Stanley *was* flat, but he got round
again."

"**Clever**!" said Mrs. Christmas. "Well!
Do all come in! Are you **fond** of hot
chocolate?"

". . . an excellent plan, I do see that. But—
Oh, he's in *such* a **state**! And with Stanley
no longer flat . . ." Mrs. Christmas **sigh**ed.
"More chocolate, Lambchops? I add a
dash of cinnamon. **Tasty**, yes?"

"Delicious," said Mrs. Lambchop.

Everyone sat silent, **sip**ping.

Mr. Lambchop felt the time had come. "May we see him now, Mrs. Christmas? We should be getting home. So much to do, this time of year."

"You forget where you are, George," said Mrs. Lambchop. "Mrs. Christmas, surely, is **aware** of the **demand**s of the season."

"I'm sorry about not being flat," Stanley said. "I did get **tired** of it, though."

"No need to **apologize**," said Mrs. Christmas. "Flat, round, whatever, people must be what shape they wish."

"So true," said Mrs. Lambchop. "But will your husband agree?"

"We shall see. Come." Mrs. Christmas rose, and the Lambchops followed her down the hall.

Mrs. Christmas **knock**ed on a door. "Visitors, dear! From America."

"Send 'em back!" said a deep voice.

"Sir?" Mr. Lambchop tried to sound **cheerful**. "A few minutes, perhaps? ''Tis★ the season to be **jolly**,' eh? We—"

"Bah!" said the voice. "Go home!"

"What a **terrible temper**!" Stanley said. "He doesn't want to meet us at all!"

"I already *have* met him once," Arthur **whisper**ed. "In a **department store**."

"That wasn't the real one, dear," Mrs. Lambchop said.

"Too bad," said Arthur. "He was much

★ **'tis** 'it is'의 단축형.

nicer than this one."

Sarah stepped forward. "Poppa? Can you hear me, Poppa?"

"I hear you, all right!" said the deep voice. "Took the Great Sleigh without **permission**, didn't you? **Rascal!**"

"The letter on your wall, Poppa?" Sarah said. "The Lambchop letter? Well, they're *here*, the whole family! It wasn't easy, Poppa! I went down their **chimney** and **scrape**d my **knee**, and then I **bang**ed it, the *same* knee, when I—"

"SARAH!" said the voice.

Sarah **hush**ed, and so did everyone else.

"The flat boy, eh?" said the voice. "Hmmmm . . ."

Mrs. Lambchop took a **comb** from

her bag and **tidied** Arthur's hair. Mr.
Lambchop **straighten**ed Stanley's **collar**.

"Come in!" said the voice behind the
door.

Sarah's Father

The room was very dark, but it was possible to **make out** a desk at the far side, and someone seated behind it.

The Lambchops **held their breaths**. This was perhaps the most famous person in the world!

"Guess what, Poppa?" said Sarah, sounding quite nervous. "The Lambchops

know *names* for our **reindeer!**"

No answer came.

"Names, Poppa, not just *numbers!* There's Dashes and Frances and—"

"Dasher," said Stanley, "then Dancer, then—"

"*Then* Frances!" cried Sarah. "Or is it *Prances?* Then—"

"**Waste** of time, this!" said the **figure** behind the desk. But then a **switch click**ed, and lights came on.

The Lambchops **stared**.

Except for a large TV in one corner and a speaker-box on the desk, the room was much like Mr. Lambchop's **study** at home. There were book**shelves** and comfortable chairs. **Frame**d letters, one of them Stanley's, hung behind the desk, along with photographs of Mrs. Christmas, Sarah, and elves and reindeer, **singly** and in groups.

Sarah's father was large and **stout**, but **otherwise** not what they had **expect**ed.

He wore a blue **zip** jacket with "N. **Pole Athletic** Club" lettered across it, and sat with his feet, in **fuzzy** brown **slippers**, up on the desk. His long white hair and **beard** were in need of **trim**ming, and the beard had **crumb**s in it. On the desk, along with his feet, were a **plate** of cookies, a **bowl** of potato **chip**s, and a bottle of strawberry soda* with a **straw** in it.

★ soda 탄산음료. 이산화탄소를 물에 녹여 만든, 맛이 산뜻하고 시원한 음료.

"George Lambchop, sir," said Mr. Lambchop. "Good evening. May I **present** my wife, Harriet, and our sons, Stanley and Arthur?"

"How do you do." Sarah's father **sip**ped his soda. "Whichever is Stanley, step forward, please, and turn about."

Stanley stepped forward and turned about.

"You're *round*, boy!"

"I blew him up," said Arthur. "With a bicycle **pump**."

Sarah's father raised his **eyebrow**s. "Very funny. Very funny indeed." He ate some potato chips. "Well? What brings you all here?"

Mr. Lambchop **clear**ed **his throat**. "I

47

understand, Mr.—No, that can't be right. What *is* the **proper** form of **address**?"

"**Depend**s where you're from. 'Santa' is the American way. But I'm known also as Father Christmas,* *Père Noel,** *Babbo Natale,** *Julenisse* . . .* Little country, way off somewhere, they call me 'The Great Hugga Wagoo.'"

"Hugga Wagoo?" Arthur laughed loudly, and Mrs. Lambchop shook her head at him.

Mr. Lambchop continued. "We

★ **Father Christmas** 영국에서 산타클로스를 부르는 표현.

✷ **Père Noel** 프랑스에서 산타클로스를 부르는 표현. 프랑스어로 'père'는 아버지 또는 할아버지를, 'Noel'은 크리스마스를 의미한다.

✻ **Babbo Natale** 이탈리아에서 산타클로스를 부르는 표현. 이탈리아어로 'babbo'는 아버지를, 'Natale'는 크리마스를 의미한다.

✶ **Julenisse** 노르웨이에서 산타클로스를 부르는 표현.

understand, sir—*Santa,* if I may?—that you **propose** not to **make** your **rounds** this year. We are here to ask that you **reconsider.**"

"Reconsider?" said Sarah's father. "The way things are these days? Hah! See for yourselves!"

The big TV in the corner clicked on, and he switched from **channel** to channel.

The first channel showed **battleship**s **firing flaming missile**s; the second, airplanes dropping **bomb**s; the third, cars **crash**ing other cars. Then came buildings **burn**ing, people **beg**ging for food, people hitting each other, people firing **pistol**s at **policemen**. The last channel showed a game show, men and women in chicken

costumes grab**bing** for **prize**s in a **pool** of **mud**.

Sarah's father **switch**ed **off** the TV. "Peace on Earth? **Goodwill** toward men? Been wasting my time, it seems!"

"You have been watching *far* too much television," said Mrs. Lambchop. "**No wonder** you take a **dim** view of things."

"Facts are facts, madam! Everywhere, **violence** and **greed**! Hah! Right here in my own office, a whole family come begging for Christmas **treat**s!"

The Lambchops were deeply shocked.

"I'm **greedy** sometimes," said Stanley. "But not always."

"I'm quite nice, actually," Arthur said. "And Stanley's even nicer than me."

"*I*, dear," said Mrs. Lambchop. "Nicer than *I*."

Mr. Lambchop, finding it hard to believe that he was at the North Pole having a **conversation** like this, chose his words with care.

"You **misjudge** us, sir," he said. "There

is indeed much violence in the world, and **selfish**ness. But not everyone—we Lambchops, for example—"

"Hah! Different, are you?" Sarah's father spoke into the little box on his desk. "Yo! Elf Ewald?"

"Central Files," said a voice from the box. "Ewald here."

"Ewald," said Sarah's father. "Check this year's letters, under 'U.S.A.' Bring me the 'Lambchop' file."

The Letters

Elf Ewald had come and gone, leaving behind a large brown **folder**.

"Not **greedy**, Lambchops? We shall see!" Sarah's father drew a letter from the folder and read it aloud.

"'**Dear** Santa, My parents say I can't have a real car until I'm **grow**n **up**. I want one now. A big red one. Make that

two cars, both red.' Hah! Hear that? **Shameful!**"

Mrs. Lambchop shook her head. "I should be interested," she said, "to learn who wrote that letter?"

"It is **sign**ed—hmmmm . . . Frederic. Frederic Lampop."

Stanley laughed. "Our name's not 'Lampop!' And we don't even know any Frederics!"

"Mistakes *do* happen, you know! I get *millions* of letters!" Sarah's father drew from the folder again. "Ah! This one's from *you!*"

"'Dear Santa,' he read. 'I hope you are fine. I need lots of gifts this year. Shoes and socks and shirts and pants and **underwear**.

And big tents. At least a hundred of each would be nice—' A hundred! *There's* greediness!"

"It does seem a bit much, Stanley," said Mr. Lambchop. "And why tents, for **goodness sake**?"

"You'll see," said Stanley.

Sarah's father read on. "'. . . of each would be nice. But not **deliver**ed to my house. It was on TV about a **terrible earthquake** in South America where all the houses fell down, and people lost all their clothes and don't have anywhere to live. Please take everything to where the earthquake was. Thank you. Your friend, Stanley Lambchop. P.S.* I would send my old clothes, but they are mostly from when

I was flat and wouldn't **fit** anybody else.'"

"Good for you, Stanley!" said Mrs. Lambchop. "A fine idea, the tents."

"Hmmph! One letter, that's all." Sarah's father chose another letter. "This one's got jam on it."

"Excuse me," said Arthur. "I was eating a sandwich."

"'Dear Santa,' Sarah's father read, 'I have hung up a **pillowcase** instead of a stocking—' Hah! The old pillowcase **trick**!"

"Wait!" cried Arthur. "Read the **rest**!"

"'. . . instead of a stocking. Please **fill** this up with chocolate bars, my favorite kind with nuts. My brother, Stanley, is

---

★ **P.S.** 추신. 'postscript'의 약어로 편지의 끝에 더 쓰고 싶은 것이 있을 때 쓰는 말이다.

writing to you about an earthquake, and how people there need clothes and tents and things. Well, I think they need food too, and little **stove**s to cook on. So please give them the chocolate bars, and food and stoves. The bars should be the big kind. It doesn't matter about the nuts. **Sincere**ly, Arthur Lambchop.'"

Mrs. Lambchop gave Arthur a little hug.

"All right, *two* letters," said Sarah's father. "But from brothers. **Count** as one, really."

He took a last letter

from the folder. "Nice **penmanship**, this one . . . Mr. and Mrs. George Lambchop! Now there's a surprise!"

"Well, why *not?*" said Mrs. Lambchop.

Mr. Lambchop said, "No **harm**, eh, just **drop**ping **a line**?"

Their letter was read.

"'Dear Sir: Perhaps you **expect** letters from children only, since as people grow older they often begin to **doubt** that you truly exist. But when our two sons were very small, and asked if you were real, we said "yes." And if they were to ask again now, we would not say "no." We would say that you are not real, of course, for those who do not believe in you, but very real indeed for those who *do.* Our Christmas wish is that you will never have cause to doubt that Stanley and Arthur Lambchop, and their parents, take the **latter** position. Sincerely, Mr. and Mrs. George Lambchop, U.S.A.'"

Sarah's father thought for a moment. "Hmmm . . . *Latter* position? Ah! Do believe. I see."

"See, Poppa?" said Sarah. "No greediness! Not one—"

"Fine letters, Sarah. I agree." There was sadness in the deep voice now. "But all, Sarah, from the same family that thought to **deceive** me with that 'flatness' story. Flat indeed!"

Mrs. Lambchop **gasp**ed. "Deceive? Oh, no!"

"Round is round, madam." Sarah's father shook his head. "The **lad**'s shape **speak**s **for itself**."

The hearts of all the Lambchops **sank** within them. Their **mission** had failed, they thought. For millions and millions of children all over the world, a **joyful holiday** was lost, perhaps never to come again.

Arthur felt especially bad. It was his fault, he told himself, for thinking of that bicycle **pump**.

Stanley felt worst of all. If only he hadn't grown **tired** of being flat, hadn't let Arthur blow him round again! If only there were **proof**—

And then he remembered something.

"Wait!" he shouted, and stood on **tiptoe** to **whisper** in Mrs. Lambchop's ear.

"What . . . ?" she said. "I can't—the *what?* Oh! Yes! I had forgotten! Good for you, Stanley!"

Rummaging in her bag, she found her wallet, from which she drew a photograph. She gave it to Sarah's father.

"Do keep that," she said. "We have more at home."

The **snapshot** had been taken by Mr. Lambchop the day after the big **bulletin board** fell on Stanley. It showed him, quite flat, **sliding** under a closed door. Only his top half was **visible**, smiling up at the camera. The bottom half was still behind the door.

For a long moment, as Sarah's father studied the picture, no one spoke.

"My **apologies**, Lambchops," he said at last. "Flat he is. *Was*, anyhow. I'**ve half a mind to**—" He **sigh**ed. "But those red cars, asking for *two*, that—"

"That was Lam*POP!*" cried Arthur. "Not—"

"Just **teasing**, lad!"

Sarah's father had jumped up, a great smile on his face.

"Yo, elves!" he shouted into his speaker phone. "Prepare to **load** gifts! Look **lively**! Tomorrow is Christmas Eve, you know!"

The next moments were joyful indeed.

"Thank you, thank you! . . . **Hooray**! . . . Hooray! . . . Hooray!" shouted Mr. and Mrs.

Lambchop, and Stanley and Arthur and Sarah.

Sarah's mother kissed everyone. Mrs. Lambchop kissed Sarah's father, and almost **faint**ed when she **realize**d what she had done.

Then Sarah's father asked Stanley to **autograph** the sliding-under-the-door picture, and when Stanley had written "All best wishes, S. Lambchop" across the picture, he **pin**ned it to the wall.

"Blew him round, eh?" he said to Arthur. "Like to have seen that!"

He turned to Sarah. "Come, my dear! While I **freshen** up, teach me those reindeer names. Then I will see our visitors safely home!"

Going Home

A crowd of elves had **gather**ed with Mrs. Christmas and Sarah to say good-bye. "**Bless** you, Lambchops!" they called. "**Thank goodness** you came! . . . Think if you hadn't! . . . Whew! . . . **Farewell**, farewell!"

In the Great **Sleigh**, Sarah's father took up the **reins**. "Ready, Lambchops?"

He made a fine **appearance** now, his hair and **beard comb**ed, and wearing a **smart** green **cloak** and cap. The famous red **suit**, he had explained, was **reserve**d for **deliver**ing gifts.

"Good-bye, everyone!" called Mrs. Lambchop. "We will remember you always!"

"You **bet**!" cried Stanley. "I'll *never* forget!"

"But you will, **dear**," said Mrs. Christmas. "You will *all* forget."

"**Hardly**." Mr. Lambchop smiled. "An evening like this does not **slip** one's mind."

"Poppa will **see to it**, actually," said Sarah. "Snow City, all of us here . . . We're supposed to be, you know, sort of a

mystery. Isn't that *silly?* I mean, if—"

"Sarah!" her father said. "We must go."

The Lambchops looked up at the night sky, still bright with stars, then turned for a last **sight** of the little red-**roof**ed house behind them, and of the elves' **cottage**s about the **snowy square**.

"We are ready," said Mr. Lambchop.

"Good-bye, good-bye!" called Mrs. Lambchop and Stanley and Arthur.

"Good-bye, good-bye!" called the elves, **waving**.

The eight **reindeer toss**ed their heads, **jingling** their **harness** bells. One bell flew off, and Stanley caught the little silver cup in his hand. Suddenly, as before, the jingling stopped, all was silence, and the

pale mist rose again about the sleigh.

Sarah's father's voice rang clear. "Come, Dasher, Dancer, Prancer, Vixen! Come, Comet, Cupid, Donder and . . . oh, whatsisname?"

"Blitzen!" Stanley called.

"Thank you. Come, Blitzen!"

The mist **swirl**ed, closing upon the sleigh.

Christmas

The Lambchops all **remark**ed the next morning on how **sound**ly they had slept, and how late. Mr. Lambchop ate breakfast in a **rush**.

"Will you be all day at the office, George?" Mrs. Lambchop asked. "It *is* Christmas Eve, you know."

"There is much to do," said Mr.

Lambchop. "I will be kept late, I'm afraid."

But there was little to **occupy** him at his office, since a **practical joke**r had left word he would not be in. He was home by noon to join friends and family for **carol** singing about the **neighborhood**.

Mrs. Lambchop had the carolers in for hot chocolate, which was greatly **admire**d. She had added cinnamon, she explained; the idea had just **pop**ped into her head. The carolers were all very **jolly**, and Frank Smith, who lived **next door**, made everyone laugh, the Lambchops hardest of all, by **claim**ing he had seen **reindeer** on their **lawn** the night before.

On Christmas morning, they opened their gifts to each other, and gifts from

relatives and friends. Then came a surprise for Stanley and Arthur. Mr. Lambchop had just turned on the TV news.

". . . and now a **flash** from South America, from where the **earthquake** was," the **announcer** was saying. "**Homeless** villagers here are giving thanks this morning for a **tremendous supply** of socks, shirts, **underwear**, and food. They have also received a *thousand* tents, and a *thousand* little **stove**s to cook on!" The **screen** showed a homeless villager, looking **grateful**. "The tents, and the little stoves," the villager said. "Just what we need! **Bless** whoever sends these tents and stoves! Also the many **tasty** chocolate bars with nuts!"

"He's blessing *me!*" cried Stanley. "I asked for tents in my letter. But I wasn't sure it would work."

"Well, *I* wrote about stoves." Arthur said. "*And* chocolate bars. But they didn't have to have nuts."

Happy **coincidence**s! thought Mr. and Mrs. Lambchop, smiling at each other.

Christmas dinner, shared with various aunts, uncles, and **cousin**s, was an

enormous meal of turkey,* yams,* and three kinds of pie. Then everyone went ice-skating in the park. By **bedtime**, Stanley and Arthur were more than ready for sleep.

"A fine **holiday**," said Mr. Lambchop, **tuck**ing Arthur in.

"Yes indeed." Mrs. Lambchop tucked in Stanley. "**Pleasant** dreams, boys, and— What's this?" She had found something on the table by his bed. "Why, it's a little bell! A silver bell!"

"It was in my pocket," Stanley said. "I don't know what it's from."

"Pretty. Good night, you two," said Mrs.

★ turkey 추수감사절이나 크리스마스에 주로 먹는 칠면조 고기.

✳ yam 고구마와 비슷한 뿌리 채소로 속이 노란빛이 도는 것이 특징이다.

Lambchop, and **switch**ed **off** the light.

The brothers lay silent for a moment in the dark.

"Stanley . . . ?" Arthur said. "It *was* a nice holiday, don't you think?"

"*Extra* nice," said Stanley. "But why? It's as if I have something wonderful to remember, but can't think what."

"Me too. Merry Christmas, Stanley."

"Merry Christmas, Arthur," said Stanley, and soon they were both asleep.

The End

스탠리의
크리스마스 모험

CONTENTS

미국 초등학생 사이에서 저스틴 비버보다 더 유명한 소년, 플랫 스탠리!

『플랫 스탠리(Flat Stanley)』 시리즈는 미국의 작가 제프 브라운(Jeff Brown)이 쓴 책으로, 한밤중에 몸 위로 떨어진 거대한 게시판에 눌려 납작해진(flat) 스탠리 가 겪는 다양한 모험을 담고 있습니다. 플랫 스탠리는 아동 도서이지만 부모님 들과 선생님들에게도 큰 사랑을 받으며, 출간된 지 50년이 넘은 지금까지 여러 세대를 아우르며 독자들에게 재미를 주고 있습니다. 미국에서만 100만 부 이상 판매된 『플랫 스탠리』 시리즈는 기존 챕터북 시리즈와 함께 플랫 스탠리의 세계 모험(Flat Stanley's Worldwide Adventures) 시리즈, 리더스북 등 다양한 형태로 출판되었고, 여러 언어로 번역되어 전 세계 독자들의 마음을 사로잡았습니다. 주인공 스탠리가 그려진 종이 인형을 만들어 이를 우편으로 원하는 사람에게 보 내는 플랫 스탠리 프로젝트(The Flat Stanley Project)가 1995년에 시작된 이후, 이 책은 더 많은 관심을 받게 되었습니다. 유명 연예인은 물론 오바마 대통령까 지 이 종이 인형과 함께 사진을 찍어 공유하는 등, 수많은 사례를 통해 시리즈의 높은 인기를 짐작할 수 있습니다.

이러한 『플랫 스탠리』 시리즈는 한국에서도 널리 알려져 '엄마표·아빠표 영어' 를 진행하는 부모님과 초보 영어 학습자라면 반드시 읽어야 하는 영어원서로 자 리 잡았습니다. 렉사일 지수가 최대 640L인 플랫 스탠리는 간결하지만 필수적 인 어휘로 쓰여, 영어원서가 친숙하지 않은 학습자들에게도 즐거운 원서 읽기 경험을 선사할 것입니다.

번역과 단어장이 포함된 워크북, 그리고 오디오북까지 담긴 풀 패키지!

이 책은 영어원서 『플랫 스탠리』 시리즈에, 탁월한 학습 효과를 거둘 수 있도록 다양한 콘텐츠를 덧붙인 책입니다.
- 영어원서: 본문에 나온 어려운 어휘에 볼드 처리가 되어 있어 단어를 더욱 분 명하게 인지할 수 있고, 문맥에 따른 자연스러운 암기 효과를 얻을 수 있습니다.
- 단어장: 원서에 볼드 처리된 어휘의 의미가 완벽하게 정리되어 있어 사전 없 이 원서를 수월하게 읽을 수 있으며, 반복해서 등장하는 단어에 '복습' 표기를 하여 자연스럽게 복습을 돕도록 구성했습니다.

- 번역: 영문과 비교할 수 있도록 직역에 가까운 번역을 담았습니다. 원서 읽기에 익숙하지 않은 초보 학습자도 어려움 없이 내용을 파악할 수 있습니다.
- 퀴즈: 챕터별로 내용을 확인하는 이해력 점검 퀴즈가 들어 있습니다.
- 오디오북: 미국 현지에서 판매 중인 빠른 속도의 오디오북(분당 약 145단어)과 국내에서 녹음된 따라 읽기용 오디오북(분당 약 110단어)을 기본으로 포함하고 있어, 듣기 훈련은 물론 소리 내어 읽기에까지 폭넓게 활용할 수 있습니다.

이 책의 수준과 타깃 독자
- 미국 원어민 기준: 유치원 ~ 초등학교 저학년
- 한국 학습자 기준: 초등학교 저학년 ~ 중학생
- 영어원서 완독 경험이 없는 초보 영어 학습자
- 도서 분량: 약 5,900단어
- 비슷한 수준의 다른 챕터북: Arthur Chapter Book,★ The Zack Files,★ Tales from the Odyssey,★ Junie B. Jones,★ Magic Tree House, Marvin Redpost

  ★ 「롱테일 에디션」으로 출간된 도서

『플랫 스탠리』 이렇게 읽어 보세요!

- **단어 암기는 이렇게!** 처음 리딩을 시작하기 전, 오늘 읽을 챕터에 나오는 단어들을 눈으로 쭉 훑어봅니다. 모르는 단어는 좀 더 주의 깊게 보되, 손으로 쓰면서 완벽하게 암기할 필요는 없습니다. 본문을 읽으면서 이 단어를 다시 만나게 되는데, 그 과정에서 단어의 쓰임새와 어감을 자연스럽게 익히게 됩니다. 이렇게 책을 읽은 후에 단어를 다시 한번 복습하세요. 복습할 때는 중요하다고 생각하는 단어들을 손으로 쓰면서 꼼꼼하게 외우는 것도 좋습니다. 이런 방식으로 책을 읽으면 많은 단어를 빠르고 부담 없이 익힐 수 있습니다.

- **리딩할 때는 리딩에만 집중하자!** 원서를 읽는 중간중간 모르는 단어가 나온다고 워크북을 바로 펼쳐 보거나, 곧바로 번역을 찾아보는 것은 크게 도움이 되지 않습니다. 모르는 단어나 이해되지 않는 문장들은 따로 가볍게 표시만 해 두고, 전체적인 맥락을 파악하며 속도감 있게 읽어 나가세요. 리딩을 할 때는 속

도에 대한 긴장감을 잃지 않으면서 리딩에만 집중하는 것이 좋습니다. 모르는 단어와 문장은 리딩을 마친 후에 한꺼번에 정리하는 '리뷰' 시간을 통해 점검하는 시간을 가지면 됩니다. 리뷰를 할 때는 번역은 물론 단어장과 사전도 꼼꼼하게 확인하면서 어떤 이유에서 이해가 되지 않았는지 생각해 봅니다.

- **번역 활용은 이렇게!** 이해가 가지 않는 문장은 번역을 통해서 그 의미를 파악할 수 있습니다. 하지만 한국어와 영어는 정확히 1:1 대응이 되지 않기 때문에 번역을 활용하는 데에도 지혜가 필요합니다. 의역이 된 부분까지 억지로 의미를 대응해서 이해하려고 하기보다, 어떻게 그런 의미가 만들어진 것인지 추측하면서 번역은 참고 자료로 활용하는 것이 좋습니다.

- **듣기 훈련은 이렇게!** 리스닝 실력을 향상시키고 싶다면 오디오북을 적극적으로 활용해 보세요. 처음에는 오디오북을 틀어 놓고 눈으로 해당 내용을 따라 읽으면서 훈련을 하고, 이것이 익숙해지면 오디오북만 틀어 놓고 '귀를 통해' 책을 읽어 보세요. 눈으로 읽지 않은 책이라도 귀를 통해 이해할 수 있을 정도가 되면, 이후에 영어 듣기로 어려움을 겪는 일은 거의 없을 것입니다.

- **소리 내어 읽고 녹음하자!** 이 책은 특히 소리 내어 읽기(voice reading)에 최적화된 문장 길이와 구조를 가지고 있습니다. 오디오북 기본 구성에 포함된 '따라 읽기용' 오디오북을 활용해 소리 내어 읽기 훈련을 시작해 보세요! 내가 읽은 것을 녹음하고 들어보는 과정을 통해 자연스럽게 어휘와 표현을 복습하고, 의식적·무의식적으로 발음을 교정하게 됩니다. 이렇게 영어로 소리를 만들어 본 경험은 이후 탄탄한 스피킹 실력의 밑거름이 될 것입니다.

- **2~3번 반복해서 읽자!** 영어 초보자라면 처음부터 완벽하게 이해하려고 하는 것보다는 2~3회 반복해서 읽을 것을 추천합니다. 처음 원서를 읽을 때는 생소한 단어들과 스토리 때문에 내용 파악에 급급할 수밖에 없습니다. 하지만 일단 내용을 파악한 후에 다시 읽으면 문장 구조나 어휘의 활용에 더 집중하게 되고, 원서를 더 깊이 있게 읽을 수 있습니다. 그 과정에서 리딩 속도에 탄력이 붙고 리딩 실력 또한 더 확고히 다지게 됩니다.

- **'시리즈'로 꾸준히 읽자!** 한 작가의 책을 시리즈로 읽는 것 또한 영어 실력 향상에 큰 도움이 됩니다. 같은 등장인물이 다시 나오기 때문에 내용 파악이 더 수월할 뿐 아니라, 작가가 사용하는 어휘와 표현들도 반복되기 때문에 탁월한 복습 효과까지 얻을 수 있습니다. 롱테일북스의 『플랫 스탠리』 시리즈는 현재 6권, 총 35,700단어 분량이 출간되어 있습니다. 시리즈를 꾸준히 읽다 보면 영어 실력이 자연스럽게 향상될 것입니다.

원서 본문 구성

내용이 담긴 원서 본문입니다.
원어민이 읽는 일반 원서와 같은 텍스트지만, 암기해야 할 중요 어휘들은 볼드체로 표시되어 있습니다. 이 어휘들은 지금 들고 계신 워크북에 챕터별로 정리되어 있습니다.

학습 심리학 연구 결과에 따르면, 한 단어씩 따로 외우는 단어 암기는 거의 효과가 없다고 합니다. 단어를 제대로 외우기 위해서는 문맥(context) 속에서 단어를 암기해야 하며, 한 단어당 문맥 속에서 15번 이상 마주칠 때 완벽하게 암기할 수 있다고 합니다.
이 책의 본문에서는 중요 어휘를 볼드체로 강조하여, 문맥 속의 단어들을 더 확실히 인지(word cognition in context)하도록 돕고 있습니다. 또한 대부분의 중요 단어들은 다른 챕터에서도 반복해서 등장하기 때문에 이 책을 읽는 것만으로도 자연스럽게 어휘력을 향상시킬 수 있습니다.

본문 하단에는 내용 이해를 돕기 위한 '각주'가 첨가되어 있습니다. 각주는 굳이 암기할 필요는 없지만, 알아 두면 도움이 될 만한 정보를 설명하고 있습니다. 각주를 참고하면 스토리를 더 깊이 있게 이해할 수 있어 원서를 읽는 재미가 배가됩니다.

The brothers **tiptoed** down the stairs.
For a moment all was silence in the **darken**ed living room. Then came a **thump**.
"**Ouch!**" said a small voice. "**Drat***! again!"
"Are you a **burglar**!" Arthur called.
"Did you hurt yourself?"
"I am *not* a burglar!" said the voice.
"Where's the—Ah!" The lights came on.
The brothers **stared**.
Before the **fireplace**, by the Christmas tree, stood a **slender**, dark-haired little girl wearing a red jacket and skirt, both **trimmed** with white **fur**.
"I **bang**ed it *twice*," she said, **rubbing** her **knee**. "Coming down the **chimney**."

워크북(Workbook) 구성

Check Your Reading Speed
해당 챕터의 단어 수가 기록되어 있어, 리딩 속도를 측정할 수 있습니다. 특히 리딩 속도를 중시하는 독자들이 유용하게 사용할 수 있습니다.

Build Your Vocabulary
본문에 볼드 표시되어 있는 단어들이 정리되어 있습니다. 리딩 전·후에 반복해서 보면 원서를 더욱 쉽게 읽을 수 있고, 어휘력도 빠르게 향상될 것입니다.

단어는 〈스펠링 - 빈도 - 발음기호 - 품사 - 한글 뜻 - 영문 뜻〉 순서로 표기되어 있으며 빈도 표시(★)가 많을수록 필수 어휘입니다. 반복해서 등장하는 단어는 빈도 대신 '복습'으로 표기되어 있습니다. 품사는 아래와 같이 표기했습니다.

n. 명사 │ a. 형용사 │ ad. 부사 │ v. 동사

conj. 접속사 │ prep. 전치사 │ int. 감탄사 │ idiom 숙어 및 관용구

Comprehension Quiz
간단한 퀴즈를 통해 읽은 내용에 대한 이해력을 점검해 볼 수 있습니다.

한국어 번역
영문과 비교할 수 있도록 최대한 직역에 가까운 번역을 담았습니다.

오디오북 구성

이 책에는 '듣기 훈련'과 '소리 내어 읽기 훈련'을 위한 2가지 종류의 오디오북이
기본으로 포함되어 있습니다.

- 듣기 훈련용 오디오북: 분당 145단어 속도 (미국 현지에서 판매 중인 오디오북)
- 따라 읽기용 오디오북: 분당 110단어 속도 (소리 내어 읽기 훈련용 오디오북)

 QR코드를 인식하여 따라 읽기용 & 듣기 훈련용 두 가지 오디오북을 들어
보세요! 더불어 롱테일북스 홈페이지 (www.longtailbooks.co.kr)에서도
오디오북 MP3 파일을 다운로드 받을 수 있습니다.

Prologue

1. What had the Mail Elves done at the Post Office?

A. They had put many letters in envelopes.

B. They had shipped gifts to different countries.

C. They had written letters to send to people.

D. They had made lists of what people wanted.

2. What are the Doll Room, the Toy Plant, and the Game Mill?

A. The names of games

B. The names of streets

C. The names of workshops

D. The names of homes

3. What is the Wrap Shed used for?

A. It is used to cover gifts in nice paper.

B. It is used to make gifts of many sizes.

C. It is used to test gifts to make sure they work well.

D. It is used to store gifts for a long time.

4. Why has the girl's father been so upset lately?

A. He has not been able to take enough naps.

B. He doesn't believe that everything is ready yet.

C. He thinks that this year's gifts are terrible.

D. He feels that no one cares anymore.

5. What had Stanley written in the letter?

A. He had written that he still needed new clothes.

B. He had written that he didn't need any gifts.

C. He had written that he was disappointed with his gifts.

D. He had written that he was bothered by his flatness.

Check Your Reading Speed
1분에 몇 단어를 읽는지 리딩 속도를 측정해보세요.

$$\frac{371 \ words}{reading \ time \ (\quad) \ sec} \times 60 = (\quad) \ WPM$$

Build Your Vocabulary

check up idiom ~을 확인하다
To check up means to make certain about something by checking it.

* **workshop** [wɔ́:rkʃap] n. 작업장
A workshop is a building which contains tools or machinery for making or repairing things, especially using wood or metal.

* **plant** [plænt] n. 공장; 시설; 식물, 초목; v. 심다; (장소에) 놓다
Plant is large machinery that is used in industrial processes.

* **mill** [mil] n. 공장; 방앗간, 제분소; v. 갈다, 으깨다
A mill is a factory used for making and processing materials such as steel, wool, or cotton.

* **fill** [fil] v. (주문대로) 이행하다; (가득) 채우다; (구멍·틈을) 때우다
If you fill an order or a prescription, you provide the things that are asked for.

take care idiom ~을 처리하다; ~을 돌보다
If you take care to do something, you make sure that you do it.

* **wrap** [ræp] n. 포장지; 랩; v. (무엇의 둘레를) 두르다; 포장하다; 둘러싸다
Wrap is the material that something is wrapped in.

* **shed** [ʃed] n. (작은) 헛간; v. 떨어뜨리다, 흘리다
A shed is a small building that is used for storing things such as garden tools.

* **gay** [gei] a. (색채가) 화려한; 명랑한, 즐거운
A gay object is brightly colored and pretty to look at.

* **pine** [pain] n. (= pine tree) 소나무
A pine tree or a pine is a tall tree which has very thin, sharp leaves and a fresh smell. Pine trees have leaves all year round.

* **cone** [koun] n. 원뿔형 열매; 원뿔 (pine cone n. 솔방울)
A pine cone is one of the brown oval seed cases produced by a pine tree.

* **lane** [lein] n. (좁은) 길; 도로, 길
A lane is a narrow road, especially in the country.

* **tease** [ti:z] v. 놀리다, 장난하다; (동물을) 못 살게 굴다; n. 장난, 놀림
To tease someone means to laugh at them or make jokes about them in order to embarrass, annoy, or upset them.

snoop [snu:p] v. 기웃거리다, 염탐하다; n. 염탐꾼; 염탐
If someone snoops around a place, they secretly look around it in order to find out things.

‡ **square** [skwɛər] n. 광장; 정사각형; a. 정사각형 모양의; 직각의; 공정한
In a town or city, a square is a flat open place, often in the shape of a square.

* **slam** [slæm] v. 쾅 닫다; 세게 치다, 놓다; n. 쾅 하고 닫기; 탕 하는 소리
If you slam a door or window or if it slams, it shuts noisily and with great force.

‡ **dear** [diər] n. 얘야; 여보, 당신; int. 이런!, 맙소사!; a. 사랑하는; ~에게
You can call someone dear as a sign of affection.

* **weep** [wi:p] v. 울다, 눈물을 흘리다; 물기를 내뿜다; n. 울기
If someone weeps, they cry.

* **nap** [næp] n. 낮잠; v. 잠깐 자다, 낮잠을 자다
If you have a nap, you have a short sleep, usually during the day.

sob [sab] v. 흐느끼다, 흐느껴 울다; n. 흐느껴 울기, 흐느낌
When someone sobs, they cry in a noisy way, breathing in short breaths.

cross [krɔːs] a. 짜증난, 약간 화가 난; v. (가로질러) 건너다; n. 십자 기호
Someone who is cross is rather angry or irritated.

lately [léitli] ad. 최근에, 얼마 전에
You use lately to describe events in the recent past, or situations that started a short time ago.

faith [feiθ] n. 믿음, 신뢰
If you have faith in someone or something, you feel confident about their ability or goodness.

growl [graul] v. 으르렁거리듯 말하다; 으르렁거리다; n. 으르렁거리는 소리
If someone growls something, they say something in a low, rough, and angry voice.

dreadful [drédfəl] a. 끔찍한, 지독한; 무시무시한
If you say that something is dreadful, you mean that it is very bad or unpleasant, or very poor in quality.

mention [ménʃən] v. 말하다, 언급하다; n. 언급, 거론
If you mention something, you say something about it, usually briefly.

frame [freim] v. 액자에 넣다, 테를 두르다; n. 틀, 액자; (가구·건물 등의) 뼈대
When a picture or photograph is framed, it is put in a frame.

except [iksépt] prep. 제외하고는
You use except for to introduce the only thing or person that prevents a statement from being completely true.

bother [báðər] v. 신경 쓰다, 애를 쓰다; 신경 쓰이게 하다; 귀찮게 하다; n. 성가심
If you do not bother to do something, you do not do it, consider it, or use it because you think it is unnecessary or because you are too lazy.

holiday [hálədèi] n. 휴일
A holiday is a day when people do not go to work or school because of a religious or national festival.

14

❖ print [print] v. (글자를) 인쇄체로 쓰다; 인쇄하다; (눌러서 자국을) 찍다; n. 활자; 출판(업)
If you print words, you write in letters that are not joined together and that look like the letters in a book or newspaper.

❖ address [ədrés] n. 주소; 호칭; 연설; v. 연설하다; 말을 걸다; 주소를 쓰다
Your address is the number of the house, flat, or apartment and the name of the street and the town where you live or work.

❖ sign [sain] v. 서명하다; 신호를 보내다; n. 표지판, 간판; 징후; 몸짓
When you sign a document, you write your name on it, usually at the end or in a special space.

Sarah

1. **Why did Sarah greet Arthur and Stanley by saying "Ha, ha, ha"?**

   A. She was laughing at a joke Arthur had told.

   B. She wanted to make Arthur and Stanley feel uncomfortable.

   C. She said it by mistake because she was nervous.

   D. She had just thought of something very funny.

2. **Why does Sarah want Stanley to go see her father in Snow City?**

   A. She thinks Stanley can convince her father to change his mind.

   B. She wants to show Stanley the letter in her father's office.

   C. She wants to prove to Stanley that her father is real.

   D. Her father is expecting Stanley to visit.

3. Why had Arthur hung a pillowcase on the mantelpiece?

A. There wasn't enough room for a stocking.

B. The pillowcase looked prettier than a stocking.

C. He didn't have a stocking to hang.

D. He could receive more gifts in a pillowcase.

4. What did Frank Smith think of the reindeer on the Lambchops' lawn?

A. He thought the reindeer were beautiful but scary.

B. He thought the reindeer were fake but amazing.

C. He thought the reindeer were small but powerful.

D. He thought the reindeer were pretty but dumb.

5. Why did the Lambchops and Sarah wait to leave until Frank Smith had gone to bed?

A. They didn't want Frank to find out what was happening.

B. They thought Frank would try to follow them if he saw them.

C. They were worried that Frank would ask to join them.

D. They wanted to make sure Frank got a lot of rest because he was tired.

Check Your Reading Speed

1분에 몇 단어를 읽는지 리딩 속도를 측정해보세요.

$$\frac{1,017\ words}{reading\ time\ (\quad)\ sec} \times 60 = (\quad)\ WPM$$

Build Your Vocabulary

stir [stəːr] v. 약간 움직이다; 젓다, (저어 가며) 섞다; n. 동요, 충격; 젓기
If you stir, you move slightly, for example because you are uncomfortable or beginning to wake up.

tiptoe [típtòu] v. (발끝으로) 살금살금 걷다; n. 발끝
If you tiptoe somewhere, you walk there very quietly without putting your heels on the floor when you walk.

darken [dáːrkən] v. 어두워지다; 우울해지다
A darkened building or room has no lights on inside it.

thump [θʌmp] n. 쿵 하는 소리; v. 쿵 하고 떨어지다; (세게) 치다
A thump is a low loud sound that is made when something heavy hits something else.

ouch [autʃ] int. 아야 (갑자기 아파서 내지르는 소리)
'Ouch!' is used in writing to represent the noise that people make when they suddenly feel pain.

burglar [bə́ːrglər] n. 절도범, 빈집털이범
A burglar is a thief who enters a house or other building by force.

stare [stɛər] v. 빤히 쳐다보다, 응시하다; n. 빤히 쳐다보기, 응시
If you stare at someone or something, you look at them for a long time.

* **fireplace** [fáiərplèis] n. 벽난로
In a room, the fireplace is the place where a fire can be lit and the area on the wall and floor surrounding this place.

* **slender** [sléndər] a. 날씬한, 호리호리한; 빈약한
A slender person is attractively thin and graceful.

* **trim** [trim] v. (가장자리를) 장식하다; 다듬다, 손질하다; n. 장식, 테두리
If something such as a piece of clothing is trimmed with a type of material or design, it is decorated with it, usually along its edges.

* **fur** [fəːr] n. 모피; (동물의) 털
Fur is the fur-covered skin of an animal that is used to make clothing or small carpets.

* **bang** [bæŋ] v. 쿵 하고 찧다; 쾅 하고 치다; 쾅 하고 닫다; n. 쾅 (하는 소리)
If you bang a part of your body, you accidentally knock it against something and hurt yourself.

‡ **rub** [rʌb] v. (손·손수건 등을 대고) 문지르다; (두 손 등을) 맞비비다; n. 문지르기, 비비기
If you rub a part of your body, you move your hand or fingers backward and forward over it while pressing firmly.

‡ **knee** [niː] n. 무릎; v. 무릎으로 치다
Your knee is the place where your leg bends.

* **chimney** [ʧímni] n. 굴뚝
A chimney is a pipe through which smoke goes up into the air, usually through the roof of a building.

front door [frʌnt dɔ́ːr] n. 현관
The front door of a house or other building is the main door, which is usually in the wall that faces a street.

‡ **greeting** [gríːtiŋ] int. (pl.) 안녕하십니까; n. 인사
(season's greetings idiom 즐거운 연말연시 되세요!)
'Season's greetings' is used as an expression of goodwill at Christmas or the New Year.

pump [pʌmp] n. 펌프; v. (펌프로) 퍼 올리다; (거세게) 솟구치다
(bicycle pump n. 자전거 공기 주입 펌프)
A pump is a machine or device that is used to force a liquid or gas to flow in a particular direction.

sink [siŋk] v. (sank–sunk) 주저앉다; 가라앉다; (구멍을) 파다; n. (부엌의) 개수대
If you sink into somewhere, you fall, sit, or lie down.

headstrong [hédstrɔ̀:ŋ] a. 고집불통의
If you refer to someone as headstrong, you are slightly critical of the fact that they are determined to do what they want.

tap [tæp] n. (가볍게) 두드리기; v. (가볍게) 톡톡 두드리다; 이용하다
A tap is the action or sound of touching someone or something gently.

proper [prápər] a. 적절한, 제대로 된; 올바른, 정당한
The proper thing is the one that is correct or most suitable.

hay [hei] n. 건초
Hay is grass which has been cut and dried so that it can be used to feed animals.

dear [diər] n. 얘야; 여보, 당신; int. 이런!, 맙소사!; a. 사랑하는; ~에게
You can call someone dear as a sign of affection.

explanation [èksplənéiʃən] n. 해명, 이유; 설명
If you give an explanation of something that has happened, you give people reasons for it, especially in an attempt to justify it.

call [kɔ:l] n. 들름, 방문; 전화; v. 부르다; 외치다
A call means a short visit to someone, especially to their home.

president [prézədənt] n. 대통령; 회장
The president of a country that has no king or queen is the person who is the head of state of that country.

amuse [əmjú:z] v. 즐겁게 하다, 재미나게 하다 (amusing a. 재미있는, 즐거운)
Someone or something that is amusing makes you laugh or smile.

sleigh [slei] n. 썰매
A sleigh is a vehicle which can slide over snow. Sleighs are usually pulled by horses.

pole [poul] n. (지구의) 극; 막대기, 기둥 (north pole n. 북극)
The North Pole is the place on the surface of the earth which is farthest toward the north.

catch one's breath idiom 한숨 돌리다, 잠시 숨을 가다듬다
When you catch your breath while you are doing something energetic, you stop for a short time so that you can start breathing normally again.

startle [sta:rtl] v. 깜짝 놀라게 하다; 움찔하다; n. 깜짝 놀람
If something sudden and unexpected startles you, it surprises and frightens you slightly.

robe [roub] n. 가운; 예복, 대례복
A robe is a piece of clothing, usually made of toweling, which people wear in the house, especially when they have just got up or had a bath.

sip [sip] v. (음료를) 홀짝거리다, 조금씩 마시다; n. 한 모금
If you sip a drink or sip at it, you drink by taking just a small amount at a time.

serve [sə:rv] v. (음식을) 제공하다; (조직·국가 등을 위해) 일하다; (특정한 용도로) 쓰일 수 있다
When you serve food and drink, you give people food and drink.

glance [glæns] n. 흘낏 봄; v. 흘낏 보다; 대충 훑어보다
A glance is a quick look at someone or something.

mantelpiece [mǽntlpì:s] n. 벽난로 위 선반, 맨틀피스
A mantelpiece is a wood or stone shelf which is the top part of a border round a fireplace.

pin [pin] v. (핀으로) 고정시키다; 꼼짝 못하게 하다; n. 핀
If you pin something on or to something, you attach it with a pin, a drawing pin, or a safety pin.

^복_습 **square** [skwɛər] n. 정사각형; 광장; a. 정사각형 모양의; 직각의; 공정한
A square is a shape with four sides that are all the same length and four corners that are all right angles.

pillowcase [píloukeis] n. 베갯잇, 베개 커버
A pillowcase is a cover for a pillow, which can be removed and washed.

* **blush** [blʌʃ] v. 얼굴을 붉히다; ~에 부끄러워하다; n. 얼굴이 붉어짐
When you blush, your face becomes redder than usual because you are ashamed or embarrassed.

‡ **extra** [ékstrə] a. 여분의, 추가의; n. 추가되는 것; ad. 각별히, 특별히
You use extra to describe an amount, person, or thing that is added to others of the same kind, or that can be added to others of the same kind.

make up one's mind idiom 결심하다, 결단을 내리다
If you make up your mind or make your mind up, you decide which of a number of possible things you will have or do.

* **sigh** [sai] v. 한숨을 쉬다, 한숨짓다; 탄식하듯 말하다; n. 한숨
When you sigh, you let out a deep breath, as a way of expressing feelings such as disappointment, tiredness, or pleasure.

‡ **joke** [dʒouk] v. 농담하다; 농담 삼아 말하다; n. 농담; 웃음거리
If you joke, you tell someone something that is not true in order to amuse yourself.

‡ **neighbor** [néibər] n. 이웃 (사람); v. 이웃하다, 인접하다
Your neighbor is someone who lives near you.

‡ **congratulate** [kəngrǽʧulèit] v. 축하하다; 기뻐하다, 자랑스러워하다
If you congratulate someone, you say something to show you are pleased that something nice has happened to them.

* **lawn** [lɔːn] n. 잔디밭, 잔디
A lawn is an area of grass that is kept cut short and is usually part of someone's garden or backyard, or part of a park.

display [displéi] n. 전시, 진열; v. 전시하다; 내보이다
A display is an arrangement of things that have been put in a particular place, so that people can see them easily.

lifelike [láiflaik] a. 실물과 똑같은
Something that is lifelike has the appearance of being alive.

reindeer [réindiər] n. (pl. reindeer) [동물] 순록
A reindeer is a deer with large horns called antlers that lives in northern areas of Europe, Asia, and America.

goodness [gúdnis] int. 와!, 어머나!, 맙소사!; n. 신; 선량함
People sometimes say 'goodness' or 'my goodness' to express surprise.

gracious [gréiʃəs] int. 세상에!, 맙소사!; a. 자애로운, 품위 있는; 우아한
Some people say 'good gracious' or 'goodness gracious' in order to express surprise or annoyance.

accompany [əkʌ́mpəni] v. 동반하다, 동행하다; 수반하다
If you accompany someone, you go somewhere with them.

hooray [huréi] int. 만세!
People sometimes shout 'hooray!' when they are very happy and excited about something.

imagine [imǽdʒin] v. 상상하다, (마음속으로) 그리다
If you imagine something, you think about it and your mind forms a picture or idea of it.

gossip [gásəp] n. 소문, 험담; 수다; v. 험담을 하다
Gossip is informal conversation, often about other people's private affairs.

nighttime [náittaim] n. 밤 시간, 야간
Nighttime is the period of time between when it gets dark and when the sun rises.

‡ unexpected [ʌ̀nikspéktid] a. 예기치 않은, 예상 밖의
(unexpectedly ad. 뜻밖에, 갑자기)
If an event or someone's behavior is unexpected, it surprises you because you did not think that it was likely to happen.

out of town idiom 다른 곳에서 온; 도시 외곽의
Out of town is used to describe people who do not live in a particular town or city, but have traveled there for a particular purpose.

* **pajamas** [pədʒáːməz] n. 파자마, 잠옷
A pair of pajamas consists of loose trousers and a loose jacket that people, especially men, wear in bed.

The Sleigh

1. How did the Lambchops feel as they waited to leave?

   A. They were concerned about whether the sleigh was safe.

   B. They were looking forward to traveling in the sleigh.

   C. They were annoyed that the sleigh was so small.

   D. They were happy that they wouldn't have to drive the sleigh.

2. What did Sarah tell the Lambchops to do before departing?

   A. She told them to be quiet.

   B. She told them not to ask her any questions.

   C. She told them to call her the Sleigh Master.

   D. She told them to fasten their seat belts.

3. What did Mrs. Lambchop think when Sarah called out the names of the reindeer?

    A. She was impressed by how unique the names were.

    B. She was pleased by how cute the names were.

    C. She was surprised at how uncreative the names were.

    D. She was shocked at how complicated the names were.

4. What happened when Sarah finally told the reindeer to go?

    A. The sleigh moved quickly down the street.

    B. The sleigh rose up high toward the clear night sky.

    C. A thick mist appeared and surrounded the sleigh.

    D. The reindeer jingled their harness bells loudly.

5. What was the journey to Snow City like?

    A. It was brief.

    B. It was boring.

    C. It was dangerous.

    D. It was tiring.

Check Your Reading Speed
1분에 몇 단어를 읽는지 리딩 속도를 측정해보세요.

$$\frac{295 \ words}{reading \ time \ (\quad) \ sec} \times 60 = (\quad) \ WPM$$

Build Your Vocabulary

‡ **aboard** [əbɔ́ːrd] ad. (배·기차·비행기 등에) 탄, 탑승한
If you are aboard a ship or plane, you are on it or in it.

‡ **bench** [bentʃ] n. 벤치; 판사석
A bench is a long seat of wood or metal that two or more people can sit on.

복습
‡ **sleigh** [slei] n. 썰매
A sleigh is a vehicle which can slide over snow. Sleighs are usually pulled by horses.

* **resemble** [rizémbl] v. 닮다, 비슷하다
If one thing or person resembles another, they are similar to each other.

‡ **roof** [ruːf] n. 지붕; v. 지붕을 씌우다 (roofless a. 지붕이 없는)
A roofless building has no roof, usually because the building has been damaged or has not been used for a long time.

* **scarcely** [skéərsli] ad. 거의 ~않다; 겨우, 간신히
You use scarcely to emphasize that something is only just true or only just the case.

‡ **contain** [kəntéin] v. (감정을) 억누르다; ~이 들어 있다
If you cannot contain a feeling such as excitement or anger, or if you cannot contain yourself, you cannot prevent yourself from showing your feelings.

twinkle [twiŋkl] v. 반짝반짝 빛나다; (눈이) 반짝거리다; n. 반짝거림
If a star or a light twinkles, it shines with an unsteady light which rapidly and constantly changes from bright to faint.

snowy [snóui] a. 눈에 덮인
A snowy place is covered in snow.

lawn [lɔːn] n. 잔디밭, 잔디
A lawn is an area of grass that is kept cut short and is usually part of someone's garden or backyard, or part of a park.

reindeer [réindiər] n. (pl. reindeer) [동물] 순록
A reindeer is a deer with large horns called antlers that lives in northern areas of Europe, Asia, and America.

fur [fəːr] n. (동물의) 털; 모피
Fur is the thick and usually soft hair that grows on the bodies of many mammals.

toss [tɔːs] v. (고개를) 홱 쳐들다; (가볍게) 던지다; n. 던지기
If you toss your head or toss your hair, you move your head backward, quickly and suddenly, often as a way of expressing an emotion such as anger or contempt.

antler [ǽntlər] n. (사슴의) 가지진 뿔 (antlered a. 가지진 뿔이 있는)
A male deer's antlers are the branched horns on its head.

clear one's throat idiom 목을 가다듬다; 헛기침하다
If you clear your throat, you cough once in order to make it easier to speak or to attract people's attention.

fasten [fǽsn] v. 매다, 채우다; (단단히) 잠그다; 고정시키다
When you fasten something, you close it by means of buttons or a strap, or some other device.

be about to idiom 막 ~하려는 참이다
If you are about to do something, you are going to do it immediately.

★ depart [dipá:rt] v. 떠나다, 출발하다; 그만두다
When something or someone departs from a place, they leave it and start a journey to another place.

‡ permit [pərmít] v. 허락하다; n. 허가증 (permission n. 허락, 허가)
If someone who has authority over you gives you permission to do something, they say that they will allow you to do it.

‡ master [mǽstər] n. 숙련자; 주인; v. 완전히 익히다, ~에 숙달하다
If you say that someone is a master of a particular activity, you mean that they are extremely skilled at it.

‡ obey [oubéi] v. 시키는 대로 하다, (명령·법 등을) 따르다
If you obey a person, a command, or an instruction, you do what you are told to do.

★ instruct [instrʌ́kt] v. 지시하다; 가르치다; (정보를) 알려 주다 (instruction n. 지시)
An instruction is something that someone tells you to do.

★ rein [rein] n. 고삐; 통솔권, 통제력
Reins are the thin leather straps attached round a horse's neck which are used to control the horse.

‡ poem [póuəm] n. (한 편의) 시
A poem is a piece of writing in which the words are chosen for their beauty and sound and are carefully arranged, often in short lines which rhyme.

★ paw [pɔː] v. 발로 긁다; 건드리다; n. (동물의) 발
If an animal paws something, it draws its foot over it or down it.

jingle [dʒiŋgl] v. 딸랑거리다; n. 딸랑 (하고 울리는 소리)
When something jingles or when you jingle it, it makes a gentle ringing noise, like small bells.

★ harness [háːrnis] n. 마구(馬具); v. 이용하다, 활용하다; 마구를 채우다
A harness is a set of leather straps and metal links fastened round a horse's head or body so that the horse can have a carriage, cart, or plough fastened to it.

‡ **mist** [mist] n. 엷은 안개; v. 부옇게 되다; 눈물이 맺히다
Mist consists of a large number of tiny drops of water in the air, which make it difficult to see very far.

swirl [swəːrl] v. 소용돌이치다, 빙빙 돌다; n. 소용돌이
If you swirl something liquid or flowing, or if it swirls, it moves round and round quickly.

복습 **startle** [staːrtl] v. 깜짝 놀라게 하다; 움찔하다; n. 깜짝 놀람
If something sudden and unexpected startles you, it surprises and frightens you slightly.

복습 **neighbor** [néibər] n. 이웃 (사람); v. 이웃하다, 인접하다
Your neighbor is someone who lives near you.

‡ **cheek** [ʧiːk] n. 뺨, 볼; 엉덩이
Your cheeks are the sides of your face below your eyes.

, **proceed** [prəsíːd] v. 나아가다, 이동하다; 진행하다
If you proceed in a particular direction, you go in that direction.

‡‡ **cheerful** [ʧíərfəl] a. 발랄한, 쾌활한; 쾌적한 (cheerfully ad. 쾌활하게, 명랑하게)
Someone who is cheerful is happy and shows this in their behavior.

Snow City

1. What did the elves look like?

   A. They had bigger ears than the Lambchops.

   B. They were shorter than the Lambchops.

   C. They wore nicer clothes than the Lambchops.

   D. They smiled more than the Lambchops.

2. What did the elves want to know from Sarah?

   A. They wanted to know why Sarah had returned to Snow City.

   B. They wanted to know if they could stop working soon.

   C. They wanted to know if the Lambchops were planning to stay in Snow City.

   D. They wanted to know if Sarah's father really wasn't going to go this year.

3. How did Mrs. Christmas know where Sarah had been?

   A. Sarah had left a note at home.

   B. Sarah had called her mother on the phone.

   C. Sarah had sent her mother a letter.

   D. Sarah had told her mother where she was going before she
   left home.

4. How did Sarah's father feel when he first heard that
   there were visitors?

   A. He was incredibly excited.

   B. He didn't care at all.

   C. He was hesitant to meet everyone.

   D. He felt bad about not greeting everyone.

5. How did Sarah's father react at first when Sarah tried
   to talk to him?

   A. He was embarrassed that Sarah had read Stanley's letter.

   B. He was touched that Sarah had wanted to help him.

   C. He was angry that Sarah had used the Great Sleigh.

   D. He was upset that Sarah hadn't taken him with her to the
   Lambchops' home.

Check Your Reading Speed

1분에 몇 단어를 읽는지 리딩 속도를 측정해보세요.

$$\frac{644 \text{ words}}{\text{reading time ( ) sec}} \times 60 = (\quad) \text{ WPM}$$

Build Your Vocabulary

mist [mist] n. 옅은 안개; v. 부옇게 되다; 눈물이 맺히다
Mist consists of a large number of tiny drops of water in the air, which make it difficult to see very far.

swirl [swəːrl] v. 소용돌이치다, 빙빙 돌다; n. 소용돌이
If you swirl something liquid or flowing, or if it swirls, it moves round and round quickly.

vanish [vǽniʃ] v. 사라지다, 없어지다; 모습을 감추다
If someone or something vanishes, they disappear suddenly or in a way that cannot be explained.

rest [rest] v. 놓이다, (~에) 있다; 쉬다; n. 나머지; 휴식
If you rest something somewhere, you put it there so that its weight is supported.

square [skwɛər] n. 광장; 정사각형; a. 정사각형 모양의; 직각의; 공정한
In a town or city, a square is a flat open place, often in the shape of a square.

roof [ruːf] v. 지붕을 씌우다; n. 지붕 (roofed a. 지붕이 있는)
A roofed building or area is covered by a roof.

tiny [táini] a. 아주 작은
Something or someone that is tiny is extremely small.

34

cottage [kátidʒ] n. (시골의) 작은 집
A cottage is a small house, usually in the country.

aglow [əglóu] a. 환히 빛나는
If something is aglow, it is shining and bright with a soft, warm light.

surround [səráund] v. 둘러싸다, 에워싸다; 포위하다
If a person or thing is surrounded by something, that thing is situated all around them.

wave [weiv] v. (손·팔을) 흔들다; 흔들리다; n. 파도, 물결; (손·팔을) 흔들기
If you wave or wave your hand, you move your hand from side to side in the air, usually in order to say hello or goodbye to someone.

ordinary [ɔ́:rdənèri] a. 보통의, 평범한
Ordinary people or things are normal and not special or different in any way.

except [iksépt] prep. 제외하고는
You use except for to introduce the only thing or person that prevents a statement from being completely true.

pointy [pɔ́inti] a. 끝이 뾰족한; 가시가 돋은
Something that is pointy has a point at one end.

wrinkle [riŋkl] v. 주름이 지다; n. (얼굴의) 주름
When someone's skin wrinkles or when something wrinkles it, lines start to form in it because the skin is getting old or damaged.

leather [léðər] n. 가죽
Leather is treated animal skin which is used for making shoes, clothes, bags, and furniture.

breeches [brítʃiz] n. 반바지
Breeches are trousers which reach as far as your knees.

tool [tu:l] n. 도구, 연장
A tool is any instrument or simple piece of equipment that you hold in your hands and use to do a particular kind of work.

needle [ni:dl] n. 바늘; 침; (계기의) 지침
A needle is a small, very thin piece of polished metal which is used for sewing. It has a sharp point at one end and a hole in the other for a thread to go through.

stick out idiom (툭) 튀어나오다, ~을 내밀다
If something is sticking out from a surface or object, it extends up or away from it.

hesitate [hézətèit] v. 망설이다, 주저하다; 거리끼다
If you hesitate, you do not speak or act for a short time, usually because you are uncertain, embarrassed, or worried about what you are going to say or do.

patient [péiʃənt] a. 참을성 있는, 인내심 있는; n. 환자
If you are patient, you stay calm and do not get annoyed easily.

straggle [strǽgl] v. 흩어져 가다; 제멋대로 자라나다
If people straggle somewhere, they move there slowly, in small groups with large, irregular gaps between them.

grumble [grʌmbl] v. 투덜거리다, 불평하다; n. 투덜댐; 불평
If someone grumbles, they complain about something in a bad-tempered way.

plump [plʌmp] a. 통통한, 포동포동한; v. 불룩하게 하다
You can describe someone or something as plump to indicate that they are rather fat or rounded.

apron [éiprən] n. 앞치마
An apron is a piece of clothing that you put on over the front of your normal clothes and tie round your waist in order to prevent your clothes from getting dirty.

bustle [bʌsl] v. 바삐 움직이다, 서두르다; n. 부산함, 북적거림
If someone bustles somewhere, they move there in a hurried way, often because they are very busy.

‡ **note** [nout] n. 편지, 쪽지; 메모; 음(표); v. ~에 주목하다
A note is a short letter.

복습 **gracious** [gréiʃəs] int. 세상에!, 맙소사!; a. 자애로운, 품위 있는; 우아한
Some people say 'good gracious' or 'goodness gracious' in order to express surprise or annoyance.

복습 **dear** [diər] n. 얘야; 여보, 당신; int. 이런!, 맙소사!; a. 사랑하는; ~에게
You can call someone dear as a sign of affection.

‡ **clever** [klévər] a. 기발한, 재치 있는; 영리한, 똑똑한
A clever idea, book, or invention is extremely effective and shows the skill of the people involved.

‡ **fond** [fand] a. 좋아하는; 다정한, 애정 어린
If you are fond of something, you like it or you like doing it very much.

‡ **state** [steit] n. 상태; 국가; 주(州); v. 말하다, 진술하다 (be in a state idiom 흥분하다)
If you are in a state or if you get into a state, you are very upset or nervous about something.

복습 **sigh** [sai] v. 한숨을 쉬다, 한숨짓다; 탄식하듯 말하다; n. 한숨
When you sigh, you let out a deep breath, as a way of expressing feelings such as disappointment, tiredness, or pleasure.

* **dash** [dæʃ] n. 소량, 약간; 황급히 달려감; v. 서둘러 가다; 내동댕이치다
A dash of something is a small quantity of it which you add when you are preparing food or mixing a drink.

tasty [téisti] a. (풍미가 강하고) 맛있는
If you say that food, especially savory food, is tasty, you mean that it has a fairly strong and pleasant flavor which makes it good to eat.

복습 **sip** [sip] v. (음료를) 홀짝거리다, 조금씩 마시다; n. 한 모금
If you sip a drink or sip at it, you drink by taking just a small amount at a time.

‡ **aware** [əwέər] a. 알고 있는, 자각하고 있는; 눈치 채고 있는
If you are aware of something, you know about it.

demand [diménd] n. 요구, 부담; 수요; v. 요구하다; 강력히 묻다
The demands of something or its demands on you are the things which it needs or the things which you have to do for it.

tired [taiərd] a. 싫증난, 지긋지긋한; 피로한, 피곤한, 지친
(get tired of idiom ~에 싫증나다)
If you are tired of something, you do not want it to continue because you are bored of it or unhappy with it.

apologize [əpálədʒàiz] v. 사과하다
When you apologize to someone, you say that you are sorry that you have hurt them or caused trouble for them.

knock [nak] v. (문 등을) 두드리다; 치다, 부딪치다; n. 문 두드리는 소리; 부딪침
If you knock on something such as a door or window, you hit it, usually several times, to attract someone's attention.

cheerful [ʧíərfəl] a. 발랄한, 쾌활한; 쾌적한
Someone who is cheerful is happy and shows this in their behavior.

jolly [dʒáli] a. 즐거운; 행복한, 쾌활한
A jolly event is lively and enjoyable.

terrible [térəbl] a. 형편없는; 끔찍한, 소름끼치는; (나쁜 정도가) 극심한
If something is terrible, it is very bad or of very poor quality.

temper [témpər] n. 성질; v. 누그러뜨리다, 완화시키다
If you refer to someone's temper or say that they have a temper, you mean that they become angry very easily.

whisper [hwíspər] v. 속삭이다, 소곤거리다; n. 속삭임
When you whisper, you say something very quietly, using your breath rather than your throat, so that only one person can hear you.

department store [dipá:rtmənt stɔ:r] n. 백화점
A department store is a large shop which sells many different kinds of goods.

permit [pərmít] v. 허락하다; n. 허가증 (permission n. 허락, 허가)
If someone who has authority over you gives you permission to do something, they say that they will allow you to do it.

rascal [ræskl] n. 악동; 악당
If you call a man or child a rascal, you mean that they behave badly and are rude or dishonest.

chimney [ʧímni] n. 굴뚝
A chimney is a pipe through which smoke goes up into the air, usually through the roof of a building.

scrape [skreip] v. (상처가 나도록) 긁다; (무엇을) 긁어내다; n. 긁기; 긁힌 상처
If you scrape a part of your body, you accidentally rub it against something hard and rough, and damage it slightly.

knee [niː] n. 무릎; v. 무릎으로 치다
Your knee is the place where your leg bends.

bang [bæŋ] v. 쿵 하고 찧다; 쾅 하고 치다; 쾅 하고 닫다; n. 쾅 (하는 소리)
If you bang a part of your body, you accidentally knock it against something and hurt yourself.

hush [hʌʃ] v. ~을 조용히 시키다; 진정시키다, 달래다; n. 침묵, 고요
If you hush someone or if they hush, they stop speaking or making a noise.

comb [koum] n. 빗; 빗질; v. 빗다; 샅샅이 찾다
A comb is a flat piece of plastic or metal with narrow pointed teeth along one side, which you use to tidy your hair.

tidy [táidi] v. 정리하다, 정돈하다; a. 단정한, 말쑥한, 깔끔한
When you tidy a place such as a room or cupboard, you make it neat by putting things in their proper places.

straighten [streitn] v. 똑바르게 하다; (자세를) 바로 하다
If you straighten something, you make it tidy or put it in its proper position.

☀ **collar** [kálər] n. (윗옷의) 칼라, 깃

The collar of a shirt or coat is the part which fits round the neck and is usually folded over.

Sarah's Father

1. How did the office look?

A. It looked big and new.

B. It looked old and dusty.

C. It looked like a very fancy workshop.

D. It looked like a rather ordinary study.

2. How did Sarah's father appear?

A. He was dressed in casual clothing.

B. His beard was neatly combed.

C. He seemed healthy and comfortable.

D. He looked quite ill.

3. What did Sarah's father say about his name?

A. He said that he preferred being called Hugga Wagoo.

B. He said that his original name was Santa.

C. He said that different people called him different names.

D. He said that only people in America called him Father Christmas.

4. Why did Sarah's father show the Lambchops what was on TV?

A. He wanted to make the Lambchops feel bad.

B. He wanted to make the Lambchops feel welcome.

C. He wanted to show how terrible people have become.

D. He wanted to show how interesting people have become.

5. What did Mr. Lambchop say about people in the world?

A. He said that most people were greedy.

B. He said that not all people were selfish.

C. He said that many people still believed in Christmas.

D. He said that violence was not a serious problem to most people.

Check Your Reading Speed

1분에 몇 단어를 읽는지 리딩 속도를 측정해보세요.

$$\frac{692 \ words}{reading \ time \ (\quad) \ sec} \times 60 = (\quad) \ WPM$$

Build Your Vocabulary

make out idiom ~을 알아보다; 주장하다

If you make someone or something out, you see, hear, or understand them with difficulty.

hold one's breath idiom (흥분·공포 등으로) 숨을 죽이다

If you say that someone is holding their breath, you mean that they are waiting anxiously or excitedly for something to happen.

reindeer [réindiər] n. (pl. reindeer) [동물] 순록

A reindeer is a deer with large horns called antlers that lives in northern areas of Europe, Asia, and America.

waste [weist] n. 낭비, 허비; (pl.) 쓰레기; v. 낭비하다; 헛되이 쓰다

Waste is the use of money or other resources on things that do not need it.

figure [fígjər] n. (멀리서 흐릿하게 보이는) 사람; 숫자; 수치; 형체, 형상; v. 생각하다; 중요하다

You refer to someone that you can see as a figure when you cannot see them clearly or when you are describing them.

switch [swiʧ] n. 스위치; 전환; v. 전환하다, 바꾸다

A switch is a small control for an electrical device which you use to turn the device on or off.

click [klik] v. 딸깍 하는 소리를 내다; n. 딸깍 (하는 소리)

If something clicks or if you click it, it makes a short, sharp sound.

stare [stɛər] v. 빤히 쳐다보다, 응시하다; n. 빤히 쳐다보기, 응시
If you stare at someone or something, you look at them for a long time.

except [iksépt] prep. 제외하고는
You use except for to introduce the only thing or person that prevents a statement from being completely true.

study [stʌ́di] n. 서재; 공부, 연구; v. 공부하다, 배우다
A study is a room in a house which is used for reading, writing, and studying.

shelf [ʃelf] n. (pl. shelves) 선반; (책장의) 칸 (bookshelf n. 책꽂이)
A bookshelf is a shelf on which you keep books.

frame [freim] v. 액자에 넣다, 테를 두르다; n. 틀, 액자; (가구·건물 등의) 뼈대
When a picture or photograph is framed, it is put in a frame.

singly [síŋgli] ad. 혼자, 개별적으로
If people do something singly, they each do it on their own, or do it one by one.

stout [staut] a. 통통한; 튼튼한
A stout person is rather fat.

otherwise [ʌ́ðərwàiz] ad. 그 외에는; 그렇지 않으면
You use otherwise before stating the general condition or quality of something, when you are also mentioning an exception to this general condition or quality.

expect [ikspékt] v. 예상하다, 기대하다
If you expect something to happen, you believe that it will happen.

zip [zip] n. 지퍼; v. 지퍼를 잠그다; (어떤 방향으로) 쌩 하고 가다
A zip or zip fastener is a device used to open and close parts of clothes and bags.

pole [poul] n. (지구의) 극; 막대기, 기둥 (north pole n. 북극)
The North Pole is the place on the surface of the earth which is farthest toward the north.

athlete [ǽθliːt] n. (운동)선수 (athletic a. (운동) 경기의; (몸이) 탄탄한)
An athlete is a person who does a sport, especially athletics, or track and field events.

fuzzy [fʌ́zi] a. 솜털이 보송보송한; 흐릿한, 어렴풋한
If something is fuzzy, it has a covering that feels soft and like fur.

slipper [slípər] n. 슬리퍼, 실내화
Slippers are loose, soft shoes that you wear at home.

beard [biərd] n. 턱수염
A man's beard is the hair that grows on his chin and cheeks.

trim [trim] v. 다듬다, 손질하다; (가장자리를) 장식하다; n. 장식, 테두리
If you trim something, for example someone's hair, you cut off small amounts of it in order to make it look neater and tidier.

crumb [krʌm] n. (빵·케이크의) 부스러기; 약간, 소량
Crumbs are tiny pieces that fall from bread, biscuits, or cake when you cut it or eat it.

plate [pleit] n. 접시, 그릇; 판; (자동차) 번호판
A plate is a round or oval flat dish that is used to hold food.

bowl [boul] n. (우묵한) 그릇, 통; 한 그릇(의 양)
A bowl is a round container with a wide uncovered top.

chip [ʧip] n. 감자칩; 조각, 부스러기; v. 이가 빠지다
Chips or potato chips are very thin slices of fried potato that are eaten cold as a snack.

straw [strɔ:] n. 빨대; 짚, 밀짚
A straw is a thin tube of paper or plastic, which you use to suck a drink into your mouth.

present [prizént] ① v. 소개하다; 주다, 수여하다 ② a. 있는; 현재의; n. 선물
If you present someone to someone else, often an important person, you formally introduce them.

복습 sip [sip] v. (음료를) 홀짝거리다, 조금씩 마시다; n. 한 모금
If you sip a drink or sip at it, you drink by taking just a small amount
at a time.

복습 pump [pʌmp] n. 펌프; v. (펌프로) 퍼 올리다; (거세게) 솟구치다
(bicycle pump n. 자전거 공기 주입 펌프)
A pump is a machine or device that is used to force a liquid or gas to
flow in a particular direction.

＊ eyebrow [áibràu] n. 눈썹
Your eyebrows are the lines of hair which grow above your eyes.

복습 clear one's throat idiom 목을 가다듬다; 헛기침하다
If you clear your throat, you cough once in order to make it easier to
speak or to attract people's attention.

복습 proper [prápər] a. 적절한, 제대로 된; 올바른, 정당한
The proper thing is the one that is correct or most suitable.

복습 address [ədrés] n. 호칭; 주소; 연설; v. 연설하다; 말을 걸다; 주소를 쓰다
The form of address is the name or title that you give someone when
you speak or write to them.

복습 depend [dipénd] v. ~에 달려 있다, 좌우되다; 의존하다, 의지하다
You use depend in expressions such as it depends to indicate that you
cannot give a clear answer to a question because the answer will be
affected or determined by other factors.

＊ propose [prəpóuz] v. 의도하다; 제안하다; 청혼하다
If you propose to do something, you intend to do it.

make rounds idiom 차례차례 방문하다; 순회하다
If you make the rounds or do the rounds, you visit a series of different
places.

reconsider [riːkənsídər] v. 재고하다; 다시 생각하다
If you reconsider a decision or opinion, you think about it and try to
decide whether it should be changed.

channel [ʧænl] n. (텔레비전·라디오의) 채널; v. (돈·감정·생각 등을) (~에) 쏟다
A channel is a television station.

battleship [bǽtlʃip] n. 전함
A battleship is a very large, heavily armed warship.

fire [faiər] v. 사격하다, 발사하다; (엔진이) 점화되다; n. 화재, 불
If someone fires a gun or a bullet, or if they fire, a bullet is sent from a gun that they are using.

flame [fleim] v. 활활 타오르다; 시뻘게지다; n. 불길, 불꽃; 격정 (flaming a. 불타는)
Flaming is used to describe something that is burning and producing a lot of flames.

missile [mísəl] n. 미사일
A missile is a tube-shaped weapon that travels long distances through the air and explodes when it reaches its target.

bomb [bam] n. 폭탄; v. 폭탄으로 공격하다, 폭격하다
A bomb is a device which explodes and damages or destroys a large area.

crash [kræʃ] v. 충돌하다; 박살나다; 굉음을 내다; n. (자동차·항공기) 사고; 요란한 소리
If a moving vehicle crashes or if the driver crashes it, it hits something and is damaged or destroyed.

burn [bəːrn] v. 불에 타다; 태워 없애다; n. 화상
If something is burning, it is on fire.

beg [beg] v. 구걸하다; 간청하다, 애원하다
If someone who is poor is begging, they are asking people to give them food or money.

pistol [pístəl] n. 권총, 피스톨
A pistol is a small gun which is held in and fired from one hand.

policeman [pəlíːsmən] n. (pl. policemen) 경찰관
A policeman is a person who is a member of the police force.

costume [kástjuːm] n. 의상, 복장; 분장
An actor's or performer's costume is the set of clothes they wear while they are performing.

grab [græb] v. (와락·단단히) 붙잡다; 급히 ~하다; n. 와락 잡아채려고 함
If you grab something, you take it or pick it up suddenly and roughly.

prize [praiz] n. 상, 상품; 소중한 것; v. 소중하게 여기다
A prize is money or something valuable that is given to someone who has the best results in a competition or game, or as a reward for doing good work.

pool [puːl] n. 웅덩이; v. (자금·정보 등을) 모으다; 고이다
A pool of liquid or light is a small area of it on the ground or on a surface.

mud [mʌd] n. 진흙, 진창
Mud is a sticky mixture of earth and water.

switch off idiom (스위치 등을 눌러서) ~을 끄다
If you switch off something like an electrical device, a machine or an engine, you stop it working by pressing a switch or a button.

goodwill [gudwíl] n. 친선, 호의
Goodwill is a friendly or helpful attitude toward other people, countries, or organizations.

no wonder idiom ~하는 것도 당연하다
You can say 'no wonder' when you find out the reason for something that has been puzzling you for some time.

dim [dim] a. (앞날이) 밝지 않은; 어둑한; v. 어둑해지다; (감정·특성이) 약해지다
If the future of something is dim, you have no reason to feel hopeful or positive about it.

violent [váiələnt] a. 폭력적인; 격렬한, 맹렬한; 지독한 (violence n. 폭력)
Violence is behavior which is intended to hurt, injure, or kill people.

greed [griːd] n. 탐욕, 욕심
Greed is the desire to have more of something, such as food or money, than is necessary or fair.

treat [triːt] n. (대접하는) 특별한 것; 기쁨; v. (특정한 태도로) 대하다; 치료하다; 대접하다
If you give someone a treat, you buy or arrange something special for them which they will enjoy.

greedy [gríːdi] a. 탐욕스러운, 욕심 많은
If you describe someone as greedy, you mean that they want to have more of something such as food or money than is necessary or fair.

conversation [kànvərséiʃən] n. 대화; 회화
If you have a conversation with someone, you talk with them, usually in an informal situation.

misjudge [mìsdʒʌ́dʒ] v. 잘못 판단하다, 오해하다
If you say that someone has misjudged a person or situation, you mean that they have formed an incorrect idea or opinion about them, and often that they have made a wrong decision as a result of this.

selfish [sélfiʃ] a. 이기적인 (selfishness n. 이기적임)
If you say that someone is selfish, you mean that he or she cares only about himself or herself, and not about other people.

The Letters

1. **Why did Sarah's father read a letter from Frederic Lampop?**
   A. He thought the letter was written by one of the Lambchops.
   B. He wanted to prove that random people were greedy.
   C. He wanted to show how kind Frederic's letter was.
   D. He figured Frederic Lampop was a friend of the Lambchop family.

2. **Why had Stanley asked for tents in his letter?**
   A. He wanted to build new homes for his neighbors.
   B. He wanted to help people who had lost their homes.
   C. He wanted to use the tents on a trip to South America.
   D. He wanted to play in the tents with his friends.

3. **What was Mr. and Mrs. Lambchop's Christmas wish?**
   A. They wished that Santa would not send any more gifts to them.
   B. They wished that Santa would prove to their children that he was real.
   C. They wished that Santa would never doubt whether the Lambchops believed in him.
   D. They wished that Santa would never cause their children to stop believing in him.

4. **Why did Sarah's father think that the Lambchops had tried to deceive him?**
   A. The Lambchops had promised to send him pictures of their family, but he didn't receive any.
   B. The Lambchops had said they liked Christmas, but they didn't seem to care much about it.
   C. The Lambchops had pretended not to be selfish, but they were expecting many gifts.
   D. The Lambchops had claimed that Stanley was flat, but he looked round.

5. **What did Sarah's father do with the photograph of Stanley?**
   A. He wrote a message on it.
   B. He had Stanley sign it.
   C. He gave it back to Mrs. Lambchop.
   D. He put it in a folder.

Check Your Reading Speed

1분에 몇 단어를 읽는지 리딩 속도를 측정해보세요.

$$\frac{1,059 \text{ words}}{\text{reading time ( ) sec}} \times 60 = (\text{) WPM}$$

Build Your Vocabulary

folder [fóuldər] n. 서류철, 폴더
A folder is a thin piece of cardboard in which you can keep loose papers.

greedy [gríːdi] a. 탐욕스러운, 욕심 많은
If you describe someone as greedy, you mean that they want to have more of something such as food or money than is necessary or fair.

dear [diər] a. ~에게; 사랑하는; n. 얘야; 여보, 당신; int. 이런!, 맙소사!
Dear is written at the beginning of a letter, followed by the name or title of the person you are writing to.

grow up idiom (사람이) 성장하다
When a person grows up, they become an adult.

shameful [ʃéimfəl] a. 수치스러운, 창피한, 부끄러운
If you describe a person's action or attitude as shameful, you think that it is so bad that the person ought to be ashamed.

sign [sain] v. 서명하다; 신호를 보내다; n. 표지판, 간판; 징후; 몸짓
When you sign a document, you write your name on it, usually at the end or in a special space.

underwear [ʌndərwɛər] n. 속옷
Underwear is clothing such as vests and pants which you wear next to your skin under your other clothes.

^복^습**goodness** [gúdnis] int. 와!, 어머나!, 맙소사!; n. 신; 선량함
People sometimes use 'goodness' instead of 'God' to express surprise.

_***sake** [seik] n. ~을 위함 (for goodness sake idiom 제발, 부디, 맙소사)
Some people use expressions such as 'for God's sake' or 'for goodness sake' in order to express annoyance or impatience, or to add force to a question or request.

[*]_***deliver** [dilívər] v. 배달하다; (연설·강연 등을) 하다
If you deliver something somewhere, you take it there.

^복^습**terrible** [térəbl] a. 끔찍한, 소름끼치는; 형편없는; (나쁜 정도가) 극심한
A terrible experience or situation is very serious or very unpleasant.

[*]_***earthquake** [ə́:rθkweik] n. 지진
An earthquake is a shaking of the ground caused by movement of the earth's outer layer.

[*][*]**fit** [fit] v. (모양·크기가) 맞다; 적절하다; a. 적합한, 알맞은; 건강한
If something fits, it is the right size and shape to go onto a person's body or onto a particular object.

^복^습**pillowcase** [píloukeis] n. 베갯잇, 베개 커버
A pillowcase is a cover for a pillow, which can be removed and washed.

[*]_***trick** [trik] n. 장난, 속임수; 마술; v. 속이다, 속임수를 쓰다
A trick is an action that is intended to deceive someone.

^복^습**rest** [rest] n. 나머지; 휴식; v. 놓이다, (~에) 있다; 쉬다
The rest is used to refer to all the parts of something or all the things in a group that remain or that you have not already mentioned.

^복^습**fill** [fil] v. (가득) 채우다; (구멍·틈을) 때우다; (주문대로) 이행하다
If you fill a container or area, or if it fills, an amount of something enters it that is enough to make it full.

_***stove** [stouv] n. (요리용 가스·전기) 레인지; 스토브, 난로
A stove is a piece of equipment which provides heat, either for cooking or for heating a room.

sincere [sinsíər] a. 진실된, 진심 어린; 진심의 (sincerely ad. ~올림)
People usually write 'Sincerely' before their signature at the end of a formal letter when they have addressed it to someone by name.

count [kaunt] v. 간주하다; 중요하다; (수를) 세다; n. 셈, 계산; 수치; 사항
If something counts or is counted as a particular thing, it is regarded as being that thing, especially in particular circumstances or under particular rules.

penmanship [pénmənʃip] n. 필적, 글씨체
Penmanship is writing done by hand, or skill in this type of writing.

harm [ha:rm] n. 해, 피해, 손해; v. 해치다; 손상시키다
If you say 'no harm,' you do not intend to hurt, damage, or upset someone or something.

drop a line idiom ~에게 편지를 보내다
If you drop someone a line, you send them a note or letter in a casual manner.

expect [ikspékt] v. 예상하다, 기대하다
If you expect something to happen, you believe that it will happen.

doubt [daut] v. 의심하다, 의문을 갖다; n. 의심, 의혹, 의문
If you doubt something, you believe that it might not be true or genuine.

latter [lǽtər] a. 후자의; 마지막의
When two people, things, or groups have just been mentioned, you can refer to the second of them as the latter.

deceive [disí:v] v. 속이다, 기만하다
If you deceive someone, you make them believe something that is not true, usually in order to get some advantage for yourself.

gasp [gæsp] v. 헉 하고 숨을 쉬다; 숨을 제대로 못 쉬다; n. 헉 하는 소리를 냄
When you gasp, you take a short quick breath through your mouth, especially when you are surprised, shocked, or in pain.

* **lad** [læd] n. 사내애; 청년
A lad is a young man or boy.

speak for itself idiom 분명하다
If you say that something speaks for itself, you mean that its meaning or quality is so obvious that it does not need explaining or pointing out.

복습 **sink** [siŋk] v. (sank–sunk) 가라앉다; 주저앉다; (구멍을) 파다; n. (부엌의) 개수대
If your heart or your spirits sink, you become depressed or lose hope.

* **mission** [míʃən] n. 임무; 우주 비행
A mission is an important task that people are given to do, especially one that involves traveling to another country.

* **joyful** [dʒɔ́ifəl] a. 기쁜, 기쁨을 주는
Something that is joyful causes happiness and pleasure.

복습 **holiday** [hálədèi] n. 휴일
A holiday is a day when people do not go to work or school because of a religious or national festival.

복습 **pump** [pʌmp] n. 펌프; v. (펌프로) 퍼 올리다; (거세게) 솟구치다
(bicycle pump n. 자전거 공기 주입 펌프)
A pump is a machine or device that is used to force a liquid or gas to flow in a particular direction.

복습 **tired** [taiərd] a. 싫증난, 지긋지긋한; 피로한, 피곤한, 지친
(grow tired of idiom ~에 싫증나다)
If you are tired of something, you do not want it to continue because you are bored of it or unhappy with it.

* **proof** [pru:f] n. 증거, 증명
Proof is a fact, argument, or piece of evidence which shows that something is definitely true or definitely exists.

복습 **tiptoe** [típtòu] n. 발끝; v. (발끝으로) 살금살금 걷다
If you do something on tiptoe, you do it standing or walking on the front part of your foot, without putting your heels on the ground.

whisper [hwíspər] v. 속삭이다, 소곤거리다; n. 속삭임
When you whisper, you say something very quietly, using your breath rather than your throat, so that only one person can hear you.

rummage [rʌ́midʒ] v. 뒤지다; n. 뒤지기
If you rummage through something, you search for something you want by moving things around in a careless or hurried way.

snapshot [snǽpʃat] n. 스냅 사진
A snapshot is a photograph that is taken quickly and casually.

bulletin board [búlitən bɔːrd] n. 게시판
A bulletin board is a board which is usually attached to a wall in order to display notices giving information about something.

slide [slaid] v. 미끄러지듯이 움직이다; 미끄러지다; 슬며시 넣다; n. 떨어짐; 미끄러짐
When something slides somewhere or when you slide it there, it moves there smoothly over or against something.

visible [vízəbl] a. (눈에) 보이는, 알아볼 수 있는; 뚜렷한
If something is visible, it can be seen.

apologize [əpálədʒàiz] v. 사과하다 (apology n. 사과)
An apology is something that you say or write in order to tell someone that you are sorry that you have hurt them or caused trouble for them.

have half a mind to idiom ~할까말까 생각하다
If you say that you have half a mind to do something, you are threatening or announcing that you have a strong desire to do it, although you probably will not do it.

sigh [sai] v. 한숨을 쉬다, 한숨짓다; 탄식하듯 말하다; n. 한숨
When you sigh, you let out a deep breath, as a way of expressing feelings such as disappointment, tiredness, or pleasure.

tease [tiːz] v. 놀리다, 장난하다; (동물을) 못 살게 굴다; n. 장난, 놀림
To tease someone means to laugh at them or make jokes about them in order to embarrass, annoy, or upset them.

58

load [loud] v. (짐·사람 등을) 싣다; 가득 안겨 주다; n. (많은 양의) 짐
If you load a vehicle or a container, you put a large quantity of things into it.

lively [láivli] a. 활기 넘치는; 적극적인; 선명한
You can describe someone as lively when they behave in an enthusiastic and cheerful way.

hooray [huréi] int. 만세!
People sometimes shout 'hooray!' when they are very happy and excited about something.

faint [feint] v. 실신하다, 기절하다; n. 실신, 기절
If you faint, you lose consciousness for a short time, especially because you are hungry, or because of pain, heat, or shock.

realize [rí:əlaiz] v. 깨닫다, 알아차리다; 실현하다, 달성하다
If you realize that something is true, you become aware of that fact or understand it.

autograph [ɔ́:tougræf] v. 사인을 해주다; n. (유명인의) 사인
If someone famous autographs something, they put their signature on it.

pin [pin] v. (핀으로) 고정시키다; 꼼짝 못하게 하다; n. 핀
If you pin something on or to something, you attach it with a pin, a drawing pin, or a safety pin.

freshen [fréʃən] v. 산뜻하게 하다; 더 쌀쌀해지다 (freshen up idiom 몸단장을 하다)
If you freshen yourself up, you wash and make yourself look clean and tidy.

Going Home

1. How did the elves feel as the Lambchops were leaving?

A. They were still confused about why the Lambchops had visited.

B. They were happy to be getting rid of the Lambchops.

C. They were grateful for everything the Lambchops had done.

D. They were sad that the Lambchops were leaving so soon.

2. How did Sarah's father appear?

A. He looked neater than before.

B. He appeared younger than before.

C. He wore his famous red suit.

D. He no longer had a beard.

3. What did the Lambchops tell everyone?

A. They said they would visit again someday.

B. They said they would send some letters soon.

C. They said they would not forget everyone.

D. They said they would not remember everything that had happened.

4. What did Sarah say about Snow City?

A. People are not supposed to know about Snow City.

B. Snow City is the best place to live in.

C. Many people travel to Snow City every year.

D. Snow City is not a memorable place.

5. What happened before the sleigh took off?

A. Arthur sang a Christmas song with Sarah's father.

B. Stanley caught a bell in his hand.

C. The elves went back to their cottages.

D. It suddenly began to snow outside.

Check Your Reading Speed

1분에 몇 단어를 읽는지 리딩 속도를 측정해보세요.

$$\frac{293 \text{ words}}{\text{reading time ( ) sec}} \times 60 = (\quad) \text{ WPM}$$

Build Your Vocabulary

¾ **gather** [gǽðər] v. (사람들이) 모이다; (여기저기 있는 것을) 모으다
If people gather somewhere or if someone gathers people somewhere, they come together in a group.

¾ **bless** [bles] v. (신의) 축복을 빌다 (bless you idiom 축복이 있기를)
Bless is used in expressions such as 'God bless' or 'bless you' to express affection, thanks, or good wishes.

thank goodness idiom 정말 다행이다
You say 'thank goodness' when you are very relieved about something.

¾ **farewell** [fɛərwél] int. 안녕히 가세요!; n. 작별 (인사)
Farewell means the same as goodbye.

복습 **sleigh** [slei] n. 썰매
A sleigh is a vehicle which can slide over snow. Sleighs are usually pulled by horses.

복습 **rein** [rein] n. 고삐; 통솔권, 통제력
Reins are the thin leather straps attached round a horse's neck which are used to control the horse.

¾ **appearance** [əpíərəns] n. (겉)모습, 외모; 출현
Someone's or something's appearance is the way that they look.

복습 **beard** [biərd] n. 턱수염
A man's beard is the hair that grows on his chin and cheeks.

^{복습} comb [koum] v. 빗다; 샅샅이 찾다; n. 빗; 빗질
When you comb your hair, you tidy it using a comb.

‡ smart [smaːrt] a. 깔끔한, 맵시 있는; 똑똑한, 영리한
Smart people and things are pleasantly neat and clean in appearance.

＊ cloak [klouk] n. 망토; v. 망토를 입다; ~을 가리다
A cloak is a long, loose, sleeveless piece of clothing which people used
to wear over their other clothes when they went out.

‡ suit [suːt] n. (특정한 활동 때 입는) 옷; 정장; v. 어울리다; ~에게 편리하다
A particular type of suit is a piece of clothing that you wear for a
particular activity.

‡ reserve [rizə́ːrv] v. 마련해 두다; (권한 등을) 갖다; n. 비축(물); 신중함
If something is reserved for a particular person or purpose, it is kept
specially for that person or purpose.

^{복습} deliver [dilívər] v. 배달하다; (연설·강연 등을) 하다
If you deliver something somewhere, you take it there.

＊ bet [bet] v. (~이) 틀림없다; (내기 등에) 돈을 걸다; n. 내기; 짐작
(you bet idiom 물론이지!)
You use 'you bet' to say yes in an emphatic way or to emphasize a reply
or statement.

^{복습} dear [diər] n. 얘야; 여보, 당신; int. 이런!, 맙소사!; a. 사랑하는; ~에게
You can call someone dear as a sign of affection.

‡‡ hardly [háːrdli] ad. 거의 ~아니다; ~하자마자; 거의 ~할 수가 없다
You use 'hardly' to mean 'no,' especially when you want to express
surprise or annoyance at a statement that you disagree with.

＊ slip [slip] v. 빠져 나가다; 슬며시 가다; 미끄러지다; n. (작은) 실수; 미끄러짐
(slip one's mind idiom 잊어 버리다)
If something slips your mind, you forget about it.

see to it idiom 반드시 ~하도록 하다
If you see to it that something is done, you make sure that it is done.

* **mystery** [místəri] n. 수수께끼, 미스터리; 신비스러운 것
A mystery is something that is not understood or known about.

* **silly** [síli] a. 어리석은, 바보 같은; 우스꽝스러운; n. 바보
If you say that someone or something is silly, you mean that they are foolish, childish, or ridiculous.

* **sight** [sait] n. 광경, 모습; 보기, 봄; v. 갑자기 보다
A sight is something that you see.

복습 **roof** [ru:f] v. 지붕을 씌우다; n. 지붕 (roofed a. 지붕이 있는)
A roofed building or area is covered by a roof.

복습 **cottage** [kátidʒ] n. (시골의) 작은 집
A cottage is a small house, usually in the country.

복습 **snowy** [snóui] a. 눈에 덮인
A snowy place is covered in snow.

복습 **square** [skwɛər] n. 광장; 정사각형; a. 정사각형 모양의; 직각의; 공정한
In a town or city, a square is a flat open place, often in the shape of a square.

복습 **wave** [weiv] v. (손·팔을) 흔들다; 흔들리다; n. 파도, 물결; (손·팔을) 흔들기
If you wave or wave your hand, you move your hand from side to side in the air, usually in order to say hello or goodbye to someone.

복습 **reindeer** [réindiər] n. (pl. reindeer) [동물] 순록
A reindeer is a deer with large horns called antlers that lives in northern areas of Europe, Asia, and America.

복습 **toss** [tɔ:s] v. (고개를) 홱 쳐들다; (가볍게) 던지다; n. 던지기
If you toss your head or toss your hair, you move your head backward, quickly and suddenly, often as a way of expressing an emotion such as anger or contempt.

복습 **jingle** [dʒiŋgl] v. 딸랑거리다; n. 딸랑, 짤랑 (하고 울리는 소리)
When something jingles or when you jingle it, it makes a gentle ringing noise, like small bells.

^복_습**harness** [háːrnis] n. 마구(馬具); v. 이용하다, 활용하다; 마구를 채우다
A harness is a set of leather straps and metal links fastened round a horse's head or body so that the horse can have a carriage, cart, or plough fastened to it.

***pale** [peil] a. 옅은; 창백한, 핼쑥한; v. 창백해지다
If something is pale, it is very light in color or almost white.

^복_습**mist** [mist] n. 엷은 안개; v. 부옇게 되다; 눈물이 맺히다
Mist consists of a large number of tiny drops of water in the air, which make it difficult to see very far.

^복_습**swirl** [swəːrl] v. 소용돌이치다, 빙빙 돌다; n. 소용돌이
If you swirl something liquid or flowing, or if it swirls, it moves round and round quickly.

Christmas

1. **Why did Mrs. Lambchop add cinnamon to the hot chocolate?**

   A. She said it was what Mrs. Christmas had done.

   B. She said she had just thought of the idea.

   C. She said she wanted to experiment with a new recipe.

   D. She said she thought all of the carolers preferred their hot chocolate that way.

2. **What did the Lambchops think about Frank Smith seeing reindeer on their lawn?**

   A. They believed it must have really happened.

   B. They assumed it must have been someone else's lawn.

   C. They thought Frank had just imagined it all.

   D. They were surprised that Frank had remembered seeing the reindeer.

3. **What did Mr. and Mrs. Lambchop think about the gifts received in South America?**
   A. They were shocked that Stanley and Arthur's letters had actually worked.
   B. They thought it was odd that the gifts matched what Stanley and Arthur had written in their letters.
   C. They didn't believe that the gifts were received because of Stanley and Arthur's letters.
   D. They were proud that many people received gifts because of Stanley and Arthur's letters.

4. **What did Stanley say about the silver bell?**
   A. He had found it on the table by his bed.
   B. He didn't remember where he had gotten it.
   C. He had taken it from Snow City.
   D. It was the best gift he had received all day.

5. **How did Stanley and Arthur feel about the holiday?**
   A. They thought it was special.
   B. They thought it was normal.
   C. They thought it felt a little empty.
   D. They thought it felt like a dream.

Check Your Reading Speed

1분에 몇 단어를 읽는지 리딩 속도를 측정해보세요.

$$\frac{489 \ words}{reading \ time \ (\quad) \ sec} \times 60 = (\qquad) \ WPM$$

Build Your Vocabulary

* remark [rimáːrk] v. 언급하다, 말하다; n. 발언, 언급; 주목
If you remark that something is the case, you say that it is the case.

* sound [saund] a. (잠이) 깊은; 믿을 만한, 타당한; v. ~처럼 들리다 (soundly ad. 깊이, 푹)
If you sleep soundly, you sleep deeply and do not wake during your sleep.

* rush [rʌʃ] n. 혼잡, 분주함; v. 급히 움직이다; 서두르다; 재촉하다
A rush is a situation in which you need to go somewhere or do something very quickly.

* occupy [ákjupài] v. ~를 바쁘게 하다; (공간·시간을) 차지하다
If something occupies you, or if you occupy yourself, your time, or your mind with it, you are busy doing that thing or thinking about it.

practiacal joke [prǽktikəl dʒóuk] n. 짓궂은 장난
(practical joker n. 짓궂은 장난꾼)
A practical joke is a trick that is intended to embarrass someone or make them look ridiculous.

carol [kǽrəl] n. 크리스마스 캐럴; v. 즐겁게 노래하다 (caroler n. 캐럴을 부르는 사람)
Carols are Christian religious songs that are sung at Christmas.

* neighborhood [néibərhùd] n. 이웃, 인근; 이웃 사람들
A neighborhood is one of the parts of a town where people live.

admire [ædmáiər] v. 감탄하며 바라보다; 존경하다, 칭찬하다
If you admire someone or something, you like and respect them very much.

pop [pap] v. 불쑥 나타나다; 펑 하는 소리가 나다; n. 펑 (하는 소리)
If something pops up, it appears or happens when you do not expect it.

jolly [dʒáli] a. 즐거운; 행복한, 쾌활한
Someone who is jolly is happy and cheerful in their appearance or behavior.

next door [nekst dɔ́:r] ad. 옆집에(서); n. 옆집 사람
If a room or building is next door, it is the next one to the right or left.

claim [kleim] v. 주장하다; 요구하다; n. 주장
If you say that someone claims that something is true, you mean they say that it is true but you are not sure whether or not they are telling the truth.

reindeer [réindiər] n. (pl. reindeer) [동물] 순록
A reindeer is a deer with large horns called antlers that lives in northern areas of Europe, Asia, and America.

lawn [lɔ:n] n. 잔디밭, 잔디
A lawn is an area of grass that is kept cut short and is usually part of someone's garden or backyard, or part of a park.

relative [rélətiv] n. 친척; a. 비교적인; 상대적인
Your relatives are the members of your family.

flash [flæʃ] n. (= newsflash) 뉴스 속보; 번쩍임; 순간;
v. (잠깐) 번쩍이다; (눈 등이) 번득이다
A flash is an important item of news that television or radio companies broadcast as soon as they receive it, often interrupting other programs to do so.

earthquake [ɔ́:rθkweik] n. 지진
An earthquake is a shaking of the ground caused by movement of the earth's outer layer.

announcer [ənáunsər] n. (프로그램) 방송 진행자
An announcer is someone who introduces programs on radio or television or who reads the text of a radio or television advertisement.

homeless [hóumlis] a. 집 없는; n. (pl.) 노숙자들
Homeless people have nowhere to live.

tremendous [triméndəs] a. 엄청난; 굉장한, 대단한
You use tremendous to emphasize how strong a feeling or quality is, or how large an amount is.

supply [səplái] n. (pl.) 용품, 비품; 비축(량); 공급; v. 공급하다, 제공하다
You can use supplies to refer to food, equipment, and other essential things that people need, especially when these are provided in large quantities.

underwear [ʌndərwɛər] n. 속옷
Underwear is clothing such as vests and pants which you wear next to your skin under your other clothes.

stove [stouv] n. (요리용 가스·전기) 레인지; 스토브, 난로
A stove is a piece of equipment which provides heat, either for cooking or for heating a room.

screen [skriːn] n. (텔레비전·컴퓨터) 화면; 칸막이, 가리개; v. 가리다, 차단하다
A screen is a flat vertical surface on which pictures or words are shown.

grateful [gréitfəl] a. 고마워하는, 감사하는
If you are grateful for something that someone has given you or done for you, you have warm, friendly feelings toward them and wish to thank them.

bless [bles] v. (신의) 축복을 빌다
Bless is used in expressions such as 'God bless' or 'bless you' to express affection, thanks, or good wishes.

tasty [téisti] a. (풍미가 강하고) 맛있는
If you say that food, especially savory food, is tasty, you mean that it has a fairly strong and pleasant flavor which makes it good to eat.

70

coincidence [kouínsidəns] n. 우연의 일치; 동시에 일어남
A coincidence is when two or more similar or related events occur at the same time by chance and without any planning.

‡ **cousin** [kʌzn] n. 사촌
Your cousin is the child of your uncle or aunt.

* **enormous** [inɔ́ːrməs] a. 막대한, 거대한
Something that is enormous is extremely large in size or amount.

‡ **meal** [miːl] n. 식사, 끼니
A meal is the food you eat during an occasion when people sit down and eat.

bedtime [bédtàim] n. 취침 시간, 잠자리에 드는 시간
Your bedtime is the time when you usually go to bed.

복습 **holiday** [hálədèi] n. 휴일
A holiday is a day when people do not go to work or school because of a religious or national festival.

* **tuck** [tʌk] v. 단단히 덮어 주다; 밀어넣다; n. 주름, 단
(tuck in idiom ~에게 이불을 잘 덮어 주다)
If you tuck someone in, especially a child, you cover them comfortably in bed by pulling the covers around them.

‡ **pleasant** [plézənt] a. 즐거운, 기분 좋은; 상냥한
Something that is pleasant is nice, enjoyable, or attractive.

복습 **switch off** idiom (스위치 등을 눌러서) ~을 끄다
If you switch off something like an electrical device, a machine or an engine, you stop it working by pressing a switch or a button.

복습 **extra** [ékstrə] ad. 각별히, 특별히; a. 여분의, 추가의; n. 추가되는 것
You can use extra in front of adjectives and adverbs to emphasize the quality that they are describing.

프롤로그

그녀는 일을 확실하게 하는 것을 좋아하는 부류의 어린 소녀였고, 그래서 그녀는 스노우 시티(Snow City)의 모든 곳을 돌아다니며, 확인했습니다.

엘프들(elves)이 자신들의 일을 다 끝마쳤습니다.

우체국에서는, 우체부 엘프들이 편지들을 읽었고, 누가 무엇을 원하는지에 대해 목록을 작성했습니다.

커다란 작업장에서는—인형의 방, 장난감 공장, 게임 공장이 있었는데—선물 엘프들이 주문을 맞추면서, 색상과 크기 그리고 스타일에 신경을 쓰고 있었습니다.

포장 창고에서는 선물들이 이제는 호랑가시나무와 솔방울로 장식된 화려한 포장지에 포장되고, 나라, 도시 혹은 마을, 도로 또는 길 혹은 거리로 구분되어, 준비된 채 놓여 있었습니다.

포장 엘프들이 그녀를 놀렸습니다. "우리를 믿지 못하는 거죠, 응? . . . 우리는 바로 이런 걸 염탐한다고, 말하죠, 아가씨!"

"헤헤!" 어린 소녀가 말했습니다. "잘했어요, 엘프들! 훌륭해요!"

하지만 스노우 시티 광장에 있는 집에서는 모든 상황이 좋지는 않았습니다.

"문을 세게 닫지 말렴, 얘야." 그녀의 어머니가 훌쩍이면서 말했습니다. "네 아버지가 낮잠을 자고 있단다."

"어머니! 무슨 일이에요?"

"그가 말하기를, 올해에는 가지 않겠다는구나!" 어머니가 흐느꼈습니다. "그는 요즘 몹시 퉁명스럽게 굴고 있지만, 나는 절대로—"

"왜요? 왜 아버지가 가지 않겠다는 거예요?"

"그들이 믿음을 잃어버렸고, 더는 신경 쓰지 않는다고, 네 아버지가 말하는구나! 분명히 모든 *사람*은 아니겠지요, 라고 내가 말했지. 당신이 가장 좋아하는 편지를 떠올려 봐요, 당신의 책상 옆에 있는 것을요! 그는 그저 나에게 으르렁거렸어!"

"아이 참!" 소녀가 말했습니다. "이건 공평하지 않아요! 정말이요! 제 말은, 모든 것이 *준비되었단 말이에요! 왜*—"

"지금은 그러지 말렴, 얘야." 어머니가 말했습니다. "끔찍한 날이야."

집의 뒤편에 있는 작은 사무실에서, 소녀는 자신의 어머니가 언급했던, 액자에 넣어져 다른 것과 함께 벽에 걸린 편지를 살펴보았습니다:

저는 평범한 남자아이예요, 납작해졌다는 것만 빼면 말이죠, 라고 편지에 쓰여 있었습니다. 사고 때문에요. 저는 새 옷을 받고 싶다

고 하려고 했지만, 엄마가 이미 그것들을 사주
셨어요. 엄마는 그럴 수밖에 없었죠, 납작해진
일 때문에요. 그래서 저는 단지 저에 대해서는
신경 쓸 필요가 없다고 말하려고 편지를 썼어
요. 좋은 크리스마스 보내세요. 아빠가 말하기
를 조심해서 운전하시래요. 해마다 이맘때면
난폭한 운전자들이 많아지거든요.

소녀는 잠시 생각했고, 어떤 생각이
그녀에게 떠올랐습니다. "흠 . . . 뭐, 안
될 것도 없지?" 그녀가 말했습니다.
그녀는 다시 편지를 보았습니다.
램찹(LAMCHOP)이라는 이름이 윗
부분에 쓰여 있었고, 주소가 적혀 있었
습니다. 그것은 "스탠리(Stanley), 미국"
이라고 서명되어 있었습니다.

1장 사라

크리스마스가 되기 이틀 전 밤, 집안의
모든 것이, 램찹 가족 중 그 누구도 움
직이지 않았지만, 무언가는 움직였습니
다.
스탠리 램찹이 자신의 침대 위에서
일어나 앉았습니다. "들어 봐! 누군가가
'Rat'이라고 말했어."
"'grat'에 더 가까운 것 같은데." 그의
남동생, 아서(Arthur)가 자신의 침대에
서 말했습니다. "거실에서 난 것 같아,
내 생각엔."
형제는 계단으로 살금살금 내려갔습
니다.
잠시 어두운 거실에는 침묵만이 흘렀
습니다. 그러더니 쿵 하는 소리가 났습
니다. "아얏!" 작은 목소리가 말했습니
다. "젠장(drat) 또 그랬어!"
"너 좀도둑이야?" 아서가 외쳤습니
다. "너 다쳤니?"
"나는 좀도둑이 *아니야*!" 목소리가
말했습니다. "어디에—아!" 불이 켜졌습
니다.
형제는 빤히 쳐다보았습니다.
난롯가 앞, 크리스마스트리 옆에는,
날씬하고, 어두운색의 머리카락에 하얀
털로 끝이 장식된 붉은 재킷과 치마를
입은 어린 소녀가 서 있었습니다.
"나는 그곳을 두 *번이나* 부딪혔어."
그녀가 말하면서, 자신의 무릎을 문질
렀습니다. "굴뚝을 타고 내려오다가, 그
리고 바로 방금 말이야."
"우리는 현관문이 *있기는* 해, 너도 알
다시피." 스탠리가 말했습니다.
"뭐, 우리 집도 마찬가지야. 하지만,
있잖아, 매년 이맘때는 말이야. . . ?"
소녀는 약간 긴장한 듯이 들렸습니다.
"사실, 나는 전에 이 일을 해 본 적이 없
어. 어디 보자 . . . 하, 하, 하! 즐거운
크리스마스 보내세요! 하, 하, 하!"
"너도 '하, 하!'" 아서가 말했습니다.

"뭐가 그렇게 웃긴 거야?"

"웃기다니?" 소녀가 말했습니다. "오! '호, 호, 호!'라고 말하려던 거야. 난 사라 크리스마스(Sarah Christmas)라고 해. 너희는 누구니?"

"아서 램찹이야." 아서가 말했습니다. "여기는 내 형, 스탠리야."

"그래? 하지만 그는 납작하지 않잖아."

"그는 그랬었지, 그런데 내가 그를 불어서 부풀렸어." 아서가 설명했습니다. "자전거 공기 주입 펌프로 말이야."

"오, 이런! 네가 그러지 않았다면 좋았을걸." 사라 크리스마스가 의자에 주저앉았습니다. "젠장! 모든 것이 다 잘못됐어! 아마도 나는 오지 말았어야 했는지도 몰라. 하지만 그게 바로 내 성격이지. 고집불통이라고, 내 어머니가 말하곤 하지. 그녀는—"

"미안하지만." 스탠리가 말했습니다. "그런데 너는 어디에서 왔니?"

"그리고 왜 너는 오게 된 거야?" 아서가 말했습니다.

사라가 그들에게 말했습니다.

램찹 부부(Mr. and Mrs. Lamchop)는 침대에서 독서하고 있었습니다.

문에서 두드리는 소리가 났고, 그다음에 스탠리의 목소리가 들렸습니다. "저기요(Hey)! 저 들어가도 되나요?"

램찹 부부는 올바른 말투에 대해 매우 신경 썼습니다. "건초(Hay)는 말을 위한 거란다, 스탠리." 그녀가 말했습니다. "그리고 '할 수 있냐고(can)' 물으면 안 된단다, 얘야. 너는 들어와도 괜찮단다(may)."

스탠리가 안으로 들어왔습니다.

"설명해 보렴, 얘야, 이 늦은 방문에 대해서?" 램찹 씨가 말하면서, 지난 번에 일어났던 놀라운 일을 기억했습니다. "내가 보기에는, 너는 다시 납작해진 건 아니구나. 요정(genie)이 다시 찾아왔니? 혹은 아마도 미국의 대통령이 전화했니?"

램찹 부인이 미소 지었습니다. "당신 정말 재미있네요, 조지(George)."

"아서와 전 잠자리에 들었는데요." 스탠리가 말했습니다. "그런데 우리는 어떤 소음을 들었고 확인하러 갔어요. 그건 스노우 시티에서 온, 사라 크리스마스라고 불리는 소녀가 낸 것이었죠. 그녀는 말이 참 많아요. 그녀가 말하기를 그녀의 아버지가 올해에는 오지 않겠다고 했대요. 하지만 사라는 제가 그에게 부탁한다면 그가 마음을 바꿀지도 모른다고 생각한대요. 왜냐하면 제가 그에게 그가 좋아하는 편지를 쓴 적이 있거든요. 그녀는 제가 그녀와 함께 스노우 시티로 가기를 원해요. 자기 아버지의 썰매를 타고서요. 그곳은 북극에 있는 것 같아요." 스탠리가 숨을 돌렸습니다. "저는 제가 부모님에게 먼저 물어봐야 한다고 말했어요."

"그럼 당연하지." 램찹 부인이 말했습니다.

램찹 씨는 화장실로 가서 진정하려고 물 한 잔을 마셨습니다.

"그럼 자, 스탠리." 그가 돌아와서 말했습니다. "너는 우리를 몹시 놀라게 했단다. 분명히—"

"가운을 입어요, 조지." 램찹 부인이 말했습니다. "우리 직접 이 손님이 뭐라고 말하는지 들어보도록 해요."

"이건 맛있네요!" 사라 크리스마스가 램찹 부인이 그들 모두에게 내준 코코아를 조금 마셨습니다. "제 어머니도 그걸 만들죠, 시나몬을 넣어서요. 그리고 약간의 쿠키들도 같이—" 그녀의 시선이 벽난로 장식에 닿았습니다. "저건 뭐죠, 저기에 붙어있는 것 말이에요?"

"크리스마스 양말(Christmas stocking)이잖아." 스탠리가 말했습니다. "파란색이 내 것이야."

"그런데 다른 것 말이야, 커다란 사각형의 것은?"

"그건 베개 커버야." 아서가 얼굴을 붉혔습니다. "내 양말은 맞지 않을 거야. 나는 정말 작은 발을 갖고 있다고."

"하하!" 사라가 웃었습니다. "너는 더

많은 선물을 원한 거겠지, 그래서—"

"사라, 얘야." 램찹 부인이 말했습니다. "네 아버지 말이야? 그가 정말로 마음의 결정을 내린 거니?"

"오, 네!" 사라가 한숨 쉬었습니다. "하지만 전 생각했어요—스탠리가 납작해진 일, 그게 정말로 그를 흥미롭게 했거든요. 제 말은, 저는 확신할 수는 없어요, 하지만 만약 아무도 무슨 일도 하지 않는다면—"

"너는 정말 착한 아이인 것 같구나, 사라." 램찹 씨가 조금 웃었습니다. "하지만 너는 사실은 우리에게 농담을 하고 있는 거야, 그렇지? 나는—"

전화벨이 울렸고, 그가 전화를 받았습니다.

"안녕하세요, 조지." 전화를 건 사람이 말했습니다. "전 당신의 이웃, 프랭크 스미스(Frank Smith)라고 합니다. 전 늦은 시간인 걸 알지만, 저는 당신의 크리스마스 정원 장식에 대해서 축하 인사를 해야만 했어요! 최고의—"

"정원?" 램찹 씨가 말했습니다. "장식이라니요?"

"썰매 말이에요! 그리고 그 실물 같은 순록! 뭐가 그것들을 그렇게 움직이게 하는 거죠? 배터리겠지요, 그렇죠?"

"잠깐만요, 프랭크." 램찹 씨가 창문으로 가서 내다봤고, 램찹 부인이 그의 옆에 있었습니다.

"세상에 맙소사!" 그녀가 말했습니다. "하나, 둘, 셋, 넷 . . . 여덟! 그리고 저렇게 예쁜 썰매까지!"

램찹 씨가 다시 전화 통화를 했습니다. "그것들은 정말로 실물 같네요, 그렇지 않나요? 안녕히 계세요. 전화해 줘서 고마워요, 프랭크."

"봤지요? 저는 농담이나 하는 그런 사람이 아니에요, 사실." 사라 크리스마스가 말했습니다. "자! 제 생각이 효과가 있을지도 몰라요, 납작하지 않다고 해도 말이에요. 제발 스탠리가 가게 해주세요!"

"북극으로?" 램찹 부인이 말했습니다. "밤에? 혼자서? 맙소사, 사라!"

"불공평해요, 스탠리 형한테만 물어보고, 나한테는 묻지 않다니." 아서가 상처 받아서, 말했습니다. "항상 이런 식이에요! 난 절대—"

"오, 헷!" 사라 크리스마스가 미소 지었습니다. "사실은 . . . 여러분 모두 갈 수 있어요. 그건 매우 큰 썰매이니까요."

램찹 부부는 서로를 바라보았고, 그리고는 스탠리와 아서를, 그러더니 다시 서로를 보았습니다.

"스탠리가 변화를 이끌어 낼지도 몰라요, 조지." 램찹 부인이 말했습니다. "그리고 만약에 우리가 다 갈 수 있다면 . . . ?"

"맞는 말이에요." 램찹 씨가 말했습니다. "사라, 우리가 너와 함께 스노우 시티로 갈게!"

"만세!" 스탠리와 아서가 소리쳤습니다, 그리고 사라도 그랬지요.

램찹 부인은 프랭크 스미스가 잠자리에 들 때까지 그들이 기다려야만 한다고 생각했습니다. "그 소문들을 상상해 봐요," 그녀가 말했습니다. "그가 우리의 순록이 날아가는 것을 본다면 말이에요."

램찹 씨는 자신의 사무실에 전화를 걸어서 야간 자동 응답기에 메시지를 남겼습니다. 그가 내일 출근하지 못할 것 같다고, 그는 말했지요, 그가 예상치 못하게 다른 곳에 가게 되었다고 하면서요.

"저기요!" 창가에 있는, 스탠리가 외쳤습니다. "스미스 씨네 집의 불이 커졌어요."

램찹 가족은 재빨리 잠옷에서 더 따뜻한 옷으로 갈아입었고, 사라를 따라서 썰매로 향했습니다.

2장 썰매

"승차하신 걸 환영해요!" 사라가 운전석에 앉아서 말했습니다.

램찹 가족은, 대형 썰매가 지붕이 없는 버스를 닮은 것처럼 여겨지게 하는 작은 벤치들 위에 앉아있었는데, 거의 자신들의 흥분을 감추지 못했습니다.

밤하늘은 별들로 환하게 밝았고, 가까이에 있는 집의 창문에서 나는 빨간색과 초록색 크리스마스 불빛이 눈이 덮인 정원과 거리 위로 반짝였습니다. 그들 앞으로는, 여덟 마리의 순록이, 달빛에 털을 반짝이며, 자신들의 뿔이 달린 머리를 뒤로 젖혔습니다.

"우리는 준비되었단다, 사라." 램찹 씨가 말했습니다.

"좋아요!" 사라가 자신의 목을 가다듬었습니다. "여러분의 안전띠를 매주세요! 우리는 곧 스노우 시티를 향해 출발할 예정입니다. 제 이름은 사라입니다—여러분은 이미 알고 있겠지만요—그리고 저는 여러분이 할 수도 있는 질문에 기꺼이 답할 것입니다. 썰매 조종사—제가 되겠지요, 적어도 지금은—의 허락 없이 제발 움직이지 마시고 어떠한 지시사항에도 따라주시면—"

"그만해!" 아서가 말했습니다.

"오, 알겠어!" 램찹 가족은 자신들의 안전띠를 맸고, 사라는 고삐를 쥐었습니다. "하나야, 준비됐니? 준비됐지, 둘아, 셋아—"

"그냥 숫자라고?" 램찹 부인이 외쳤습니다. "아니, 우리는 그토록 사랑스러운 순록 이름을 알고 있는데! 대셔(Dasher), 댄서(Dancer), 프랜서(Prancer), 빅센(Vixen)—"

"코멧(Comet), 큐피드(Cupid), 돈더(Donder), 블리츤(Blitzen)!" 아서가 소리쳤습니다. "그것들은 우리가 알고 있는 시에서 나왔어!"

"그것들은 정말 좋은 이름들이네!" 사라가 말했습니다. "하나부터 여덟까지, 준비됐니?"

순록이 땅을 차며, 자신들의 마구에 달린 종을 딸랑거렸습니다.

"지금이야!" 사라가 말했습니다.

딸랑거리는 소리가 갑자기 멈췄고, 무거운 침묵이 내려앉았습니다.

이제는 썰매 주위로, 은빛의 안개가 떠오르고, 소용돌이쳤습니다. 깜짝 놀란 램찹 가족은 안개 너머로는 아무것도 볼 수 없었습니다. 자신들의 집이나 그들 이웃의 집, 반짝이는 크리스마스 불빛, 위에서 반짝이는 별들마저도 볼 수 없었지요. 사방에는, 그들의 뺨에 차갑게 느껴지는, 은빛의 안개만 있었습니다.

"이게 뭐니, 사라?" 램찹 부인이 외쳤습니다. "우리는 스노우 시티로 가지 않는 거니?"

사라의 목소리가 안개를 뚫고 명랑하게 들렸습니다. "우리는 이동했어요. 우리는 도착했어요!"

3장 스노우 시티

안개 너머로, 흥분한 목소리가 커졌습니다. "사라가 돌아왔어! . . . 낯선 사람들과 함께! 거대한 사람들이야! . . . 그녀는 어디에 갔었던 거지?"

"아빠의 엘프들이에요." 사라의 목소리가 말했습니다. 그녀가 말하는 사이, 안개가 소용돌이치더니, 그것이 나타났던 것처럼 갑자기 사라졌습니다. 그들 위로는, 다시 별들이 환하게 반짝였습니다.

썰매는 이제 예쁜 빨간 지붕을 단 집 앞에 있는, 눈이 쌓인 광장 안에 내려앉았습니다. 광장 주변으로는 모두 작은 오두막집들이 있었고, 그 창문들은 불빛으로 환했습니다.

엘프들이 썰매를 에워쌌습니다. "저 사람들은 도대체 누구야?" . . . "우리가 들은 말이, 정말일까?" . . . "사라에게 물어보자! 그녀는 알 거야!"

램찹 가족은 미소 지었고 손을 흔들었습니다. 엘프들은 평범한 남자와 여자처럼 보였는데, 그들이 뾰족한 귀, 그리고 매우 쭈글쭈글한 얼굴에, 단지 아서의 반밖에 오지 않는 것만 제외한다면 말이에요. 모두 도구와 바늘이 튀어나온 넉넉한 주머니가 달린 가죽 반바지 혹은 치마를 입고 있었습니다.

"사라 아가씨!" 목소리가 말했습니다.

"그게 사실인가요? 그가 올해에는 가지 않을 거라는 것이요?"

사라는 망설였습니다. "흠, 그럴지도 요 . . . 하지만 아마도 램찹 가족이 여기 있으니 . . . 인내심을 가져 주세요. 제발, 집으로 가세요!"

엘프들이 터덜터덜 자신들의 오두막집으로 떠나며, 투덜거렸습니다. "가지 않는다고?" . . . "하! 우리가 그 모든 일을 다 한 다음에?" . . . "무슨 참이라고?" "나는 다른 곳에서 일해야 하겠어, 그런데 어디에서 말이야?"

앞치마를 두른 통통한 여인이 빨간 지붕을 단 집에서 급히 나왔습니다. "사라! 너 괜찮니? 그렇게 나가버리다니! 비록 우리가 네 쪽지를 찾기는 했지만. 맙소사! 이 사람들이 모두 램찹 가족이니, 애야?"

"전 괜찮아요, 엄마!" 사라가 말했습니다. "그들은 스탠리가 혼자 오도록 하지 않았어요. 저기, 저 애가 스탠리예요. 다른 애는 아서예요. 스탠리는 납작하긴 했었는데, 그가 다시 둥글게 변했어요."

"기발하구나!" 크리스마스 부인이 말했습니다. "뭐! 모두 안으로 들어오세요! 코코아를 좋아하나요?"

". . . 훌륭한 계획이구나, 나도 그건 알겠어. 하지만—오, 그는 정말이지 흥분

하고 있어! 그리고 스탠리가 더는 납작하지도 않고 . . ." 크리스마스 부인이 한숨 쉬었습니다. "램찹 가족, 코코아 더 마실래요? 전 약간의 시나몬을 넣었죠. 맛있죠, 네?"

"맛있네요." 램찹 부인이 말했습니다.

모든 사람이 조용히 앉아서, 홀짝이며 마셨습니다.

램찹 씨는 때가 되었다고 생각했습니다. "우리가 이제 그를 만나도 될까요, 크리스마스 부인? 우리는 집에도 가야 하고요. 너무나 할 일이 많지요, 이맘때는."

"당신은 지금 당신이 어디에 있는지 잊었어요, 조지." 램찹 부인이 말했습니다. "크리스마스 부인은, 분명히, 이 기간이 주는 부담에 대해서는 잘 알고 있겠지요."

"납작하지 않아서 죄송해요." 스탠리가 말했습니다. "그런데, 저는 그 일에 대해 지겨워졌거든요."

"사과할 필요 없단다." 크리스마스 부인이 말했습니다. "납작하든, 둥글거나, 아무 형태로든, 사람들은 자신들이 원하는 어떤 형태로 있어야 하지."

"정말 맞는 말이에요." 램찹 부인이 말했습니다. "하지만 부인의 남편도 동의할까요?"

"우리는 알게 되겠지요. 오세요." 크리스마스 부인이 일어났고, 램찹 가족은 그녀를 따라서 복도로 갔습니다.

크리스마스 부인이 문을 두드렸습니다. "손님이에요, 여보! 미국에서 왔어요."

"그들을 돌려보내요!" 낮은 목소리가 말했습니다.

"선생님?" 램찹 씨가 쾌활하게 들리려고 노력했습니다. "단지 몇 분만 시간을 내줄 수는 없나요, 혹시? '즐기기 위한 계절이다'라는 말도 있잖아요? 우리는—"

"흥!" 목소리가 말했습니다. "집에나 가시오!"

"저 형편없는 태도라니!" 스탠리가 말했습니다. "그는 전혀 우리를 만나고 싶어 하지 않아요!"

"나는 이미 그를 한번 만났던 적이 있어요." 아서가 속삭였습니다. "백화점에서요."

"그건 진짜가 아니란다, 얘야." 램찹 부인이 말했습니다.

"안 됐네요." 아서가 말했습니다. "그는 이 사람보다 훨씬 더 친절했거든요."

사라가 앞으로 나섰습니다. "아빠? 제 말 들리세요, 아빠?"

"네 목소리 아주 잘 들린다, 그래!" 낮은 목소리가 말했습니다. "위대한 썰매를 허락도 없이 가져갔지, 그렇지 않니? 이 악동 같은 녀석아!"

"아빠의 방 벽에 걸린 편지요, 아빠?"

사라가 말했습니다. "램참이 쓴 편지 있잖아요? 뭐, 그들이 여기에 왔어요, 가족 전부가요! 그건 쉬운 일이 아니었어요, 아빠! 전 그들의 굴뚝을 내려가다가 제 무릎을 긁혔고, 그다음에는 그걸 부딪혔어요, 똑같은 무릎을요, 그때 제가—"

"**사라!**" 목소리가 말했습니다.

사라는 조용해졌고, 그리고 다른 모든 사람도 마찬가지였습니다.

"그 납작한 아이 말이지, 응?" 목소리가 말했습니다. "흐으음 . . ."

램참 부인은 자신의 가방에서 빗을 꺼냈고 아서의 머리카락을 정리했습니다. 램참 씨는 스탠리의 옷깃을 바로 했지요.

"들어오시오!" 문 뒤에서 나는 목소리가 말했습니다.

4장 사라의 아버지

그 방은 몹시 어두웠지만, 한편에 있는 책상과 그 뒤에 앉은 사람을 알아보는 것은 가능했습니다.

램참 가족은 숨을 죽였습니다. 이 사람은 아마도 세상에서 가장 유명한 사람일 것입니다!

"아빠, 맞춰 볼래요?" 사라가 조금 긴장한 것처럼 들리면서, 말했습니다. "램참 가족은 우리 순록을 위한 이름을 알고 있어요!"

아무 대답도 나오지 않았습니다.

"이름이 있어요, 아빠, 단순히 숫자가 아니라요! 대쉬스(Dashes)와 프란시스(Frances) 그리고—"

"대셔." 스탠리가 말했습니다. "그다음 댄서, 그리고는—"

"그다음이 프란시스야!" 사라가 외쳤습니다. "아니면 프랜스(Prances)인가? 그리고—"

"이건, 시간 낭비야!" 책상 뒤에 있는 형체가 말했습니다. 하지만 그때 전원이 딸깍 하는 소리를 냈고, 불이 켜졌습니다.

램참 가족은 쳐다보았습니다.

한쪽 구석에 있는 대형 TV와 책상 위에 있는 스피커 박스를 제외한다면, 그 방은 집에 있는 램참 씨의 서재와 무척 비슷했습니다. 책꽂이와 안락한 의자가 있었습니다. 그것들 가운데 하나가 스탠리의 것인, 액자에 넣어진 편지들이 책상 뒤로 크리스마스 부인, 사라, 그리고 엘프들과 순록이 혼자 그리고 단체로 찍은 사진과 함께 걸려 있었습니다.

사라의 아버지는 크고 통통했지만, 그 외에는 그들이 예상했던 것과 달랐습니다.

그는 "북극 체육 클럽"이라고 글자가

적힌 파란 집업 재킷을 입었고, 보풀이 일어난 갈색 슬리퍼를 신은 발을, 책상 위에 올린 채, 앉아 있었습니다. 그의 긴 하얀 머리카락과 수염은 다듬을 필요가 있었고, 수염에는 과자 부스러기가 떨어져 있었습니다. 책상 위에는, 그의 발 옆으로, 쿠키가 담긴 접시, 감자 칩이 담긴 그릇, 그리고 빨대가 꽂힌 딸기 맛 탄산음료 병이 있었습니다.

"조지 램찹입니다, 선생님." 램찹 씨가 말했습니다. "좋은 저녁이네요. 제 아내인 해리엇(Harriet)과 우리 아들, 스탠리와 아서를 소개해도 괜찮을까요?"

"안녕하시오." 사라의 아버지가 그의 탄산음료를 조금 마셨습니다. "당신들 가운데 누구든 스탠리인 사람은, 앞으로 나와서, 돌아봐요."

스탠리가 앞으로 나왔고 한번 돌았습니다.

"너는 둥글잖아, 얘야!"

"제가 그를 불어서 키웠어요." 아서가 말했습니다. "자전거 공기 주입 펌프로요."

사라의 아버지가 자신의 눈썹을 치켜 세웠습니다. "정말 웃기는군. 정말 웃기는 일이야." 그는 감자 칩을 조금 먹었습니다. "뭐? 왜 당신들 모두가 여기에 온 거지?"

램찹 씨가 자신의 목을 가다듬었습니다. "제가 이해하기로는, 선생님— 아

니지, 그건 옳지 않겠네요. 무엇이 정말 올바른 호칭인가요?"

"당신들이 어디에서 왔는지에 따라 다르겠지. '산타'는 미국식이지. 하지만 난 또한 파더 크리스마스(Father Christmas), 페어 노엘(*Père Noel*), 바보 나탈리(*Babbo Natale*), 율레니센(*Juelnisse*)이라고도 하지 . . . 어딘가에 멀리 떨어져 있는, 작은 국가에서는 사람들은 나를 '위대한 후가 와구(The Great Hugga Wagoo)라고 부르고."

"후가 와구라고?" 아서가 큰소리로 웃었고, 램찹 부인이 그에게 그녀의 고개를 저어 보였습니다.

램찹 씨가 계속 말했습니다. "우리가 알고 있기로는, 선생님—산타라고 제가 불러도 될까요?—당신이 올해에는 돌아다니지 않겠다고 했다면서요. 우리는 당신에게 다시 고려해달라고 부탁하려고 여기에 왔습니다."

"다시 고려하라고?" 사라의 아버지가 말했습니다. "최근에 일들이 돌아가는 꼴을 보고도? 하! 당신들이 직접 보라고!"

구석에 있는 대형 TV이 딸깍 하며 켜졌고, 그는 이 채널에서 저 채널로 바꿨습니다.

첫 번째 채널은 전투함이 불이 붙은 미사일을 발사하는 모습을; 두 번째는, 비행기가 폭탄을 떨어트리는 모습을;

세 번째는 차들이 충돌하는 모습을 보여 주었습니다. 그다음에는 건물들이 불에 탔고, 사람들이 음식을 구걸하고, 사람들이 서로를 때리고, 사람들이 경찰에게 총을 쏘았습니다. 마지막 채널에서는 게임 쇼를 보여 주었는데, 닭 분장을 한 남자들과 여자들이 진흙 웅덩이 안에서 상품을 잡으려고 했습니다.

사라의 아버지가 전원을 눌러 TV를 껐습니다. "지구에 평화를? 사람들에게 착한 마음을? 보기에는, 내 시간만 낭비하는 것 같군요!"

"당신은 텔레비전을 *지나치게* 많이 보고 있어요." 램찹 부인이 말했습니다. "당신이 상황에 대해서 어두운 관점을 갖게 된 것도 놀랍지 않네요."

"사실은 사실이지요, 부인! 모든 곳에, 폭력과 탐욕만! 하! 바로 여기 내 사무실에도, 가족 전체가 와서 크리스마스 선물을 구걸하고 있고요!"

램찹 가족은 몹시 놀랐습니다.

"전 가끔 욕심을 부리곤 해요." 스탠리가 말했습니다. "하지만 항상 그렇지는 않아요."

"저도 꽤 착한 편이에요, 사실." 아서가 말했습니다. "그리고 스탠리 형은 나보다 훨씬 더 착해요."

"저라고 해야지, 얘야." 램찹 부인이 말했습니다. "저보다는 더 착해요."

램찹 씨는, 그가 북극에서 이런 대화를 나누고 있다는 것을 믿기 어려워하면서, 조심스럽게 그가 할 말을 골랐습니다.

"당신은 우리를 잘못 판단하고 있어요, 선생님." 그가 말했습니다. "분명 많은 폭력이 세상에 있고, 이기심도 있지요. 하지만 모두 그렇지는 않아요—우리 램찹은, 예를 들자면—"

"하! 다르다고, 당신들이?" 사라의 아버지가 자기 책상 위에 있는 작은 상자에 대고 말했습니다. "이봐! 이왈드(Ewald) 엘프?"

"중앙 정보국입니다." 상자에서 나온 목소리가 말했습니다.

"이왈드." 사라의 아버지가 말했습니다. "'미국'이라는 부분에 있는, 올해의 편지들을 확인해 봐. 내게 '램찹' 파일을 가져와 보라고."

5장 편지들

엘프 이왈드가 왔다가면서, 큰 갈색 서류철을 두고 갔습니다.

"욕심을 부리지 않는다고, 램찹 가족이? 우리 한번 보자고!" 사라의 아버지가 서류철에서 편지 한 장을 뺐고 그것을 큰소리로 읽었습니다.

"산타 할아버지께, 제 부모님이 제가 자랄 때까지 진짜 자동차를 가질 수 없다고 말하셨어요. 저는 그걸 지금 원해요. 크고 빨간 것을요. 차 두 대로 해주세요, 둘 다 빨간색으로요.' 하! 그거 들었지? 창피한 줄 알라고!"

램찹 부인이 자신의 고개를 저었습니다. "저는 관심을 가져야겠네요." 그녀가 말했습니다. "누가 그 편지를 썼는지 알 수 있을까요?"

"그건 서명이 되었는데—흐으음 . . . 프레드릭(Frederic). 프레드릭 램팝(Frederic Lampop)이요."

스탠리가 웃었습니다. "우리의 이름은 '램팝'이 아니에요! 그리고 우리는 프레드릭이라는 사람은 알지도 못한다고요!"

"실수는 일어나기 마련이지, 알다시피! 나는 수백만 통의 편지를 받는다고!" 사라의 아버지가 서류철에서 다시 편지를 뽑았습니다. "아! 이것은 너한테서 온 거야!"

"'산타 할아버지께,' 그가 읽었습니다. '저는 할아버지가 잘 계시기를 바라요. 전 올해 많은 선물이 필요해요. 신발과 양말 그리고 셔츠와 바지 그리고 속옷. 또 대형 텐트도요. 적어도 각각 수백 개씩 있다면 좋겠어요—' 수백 개라니! 탐욕이 여기 있구나!"

"좀 지나치기는 한 것 같구나, 스탠리." 램찹 씨가 말했습니다. "그리고 도대체, 왜 텐트가 필요하니?"

"알게 되실 거예요." 스탠리가 말했습니다.

사라의 아버지가 계속 읽었습니다. "'. . . 각각 수백 개씩 있다면 좋겠어요. 하지만 제 집으로 가져다주진 마세요. TV에 남미에서 심각한 지진이 일어났고 그곳의 모든 집이 무너졌고, 사람들이 모든 자신들의 옷을 잃고 살 곳이 없다는 것을 보여줬어요. 제발 모든 것을 지진이 일어난 곳에 가져다주세요. 고맙습니다. 당신의 친구, 스탠리 램찹. 추신. 전 제 옛날 옷들을 보내려고 했지만, 그것들은 대부분 제가 납작해졌을 때 입었던 거라 다른 사람들에게는 맞지 않을 것 같았어요.'"

"정말 잘했다, 스탠리!" 램찹 부인이 말했습니다. "좋은 생각이야, 텐트라니."

"음! 편지 하나, 그게 끝이오." 사라의 아버지가 다른 편지를 골랐습니다. "이건 위에 잼이 묻었어."

"죄송해요." 아서가 말했습니다. "전 샌드위치를 먹고 있었어요."

"'산타 할아버지께,' 사라의 아버지가 읽었습니다. '전 양말 대신 베개 커버를 걸어 두었어요—' 하! 오래된 베개 커버 수법이지!"

"잠깐!" 아서가 외쳤습니다. "나머지도 읽어 보세요!"

"'. . . 양말 대신에요. 제발 이걸 제가 가장 좋아하는 견과류가 든 종류의 초콜릿 바로 채워 주세요. 제 형, 스탠리가, 지진에 대해서, 그리고 그곳 사람들이 얼마나 옷과 텐트 그리고 물건들이 필요한지에 대해 할아버지께 편지를 쓰고 있어요. 뭐, 저는 그들이 음식도 필요할 것 같아요, 그리고 요리할 작은 화로도요. 그러니 제발 그들에게 초콜릿 바, 그리고 음식과 화로를 갖다 주세요. 초콜릿 바는 크기가 커야만 해요. 견과류는 들어있지 않아도 괜찮아요. 진정한 친구, 아서 램찹.'"

램찹 부인이 아서를 가볍게 안아주었습니다.

"좋아, 두 장의 편지." 사라의 아버지가 말했습니다. "하지만 형제에게서 온 거지. 사실은, 하나로 쳐야 한다고."

그는 서류철에서 마지막 편지를 꺼냈습니다. "훌륭한 서체군, 이건 . . . 램찹 부부가 쓴 거로군! 이게 바로 놀랄 일이지!"

"글쎄요, 왜 안 되겠어요? 램찹 부인이 말했습니다.

램찹 씨가 말했습니다. "나쁜 의도는 아니에요. 음, 그냥 편지를 쓴 거예요?"

그들의 편지가 읽혔습니다.

"'산타 할아버지께: 아마도 선생님은 단지 아이들에게서만 편지가 오길 기대할 수도 있겠지요. 사람들이 나이가 들면서 그들은 종종 선생님이 정말로 존재하는지를 의심하기 시작하니까요. 하지만 우리의 두 아들이 아주 어렸고, 당신이 진짜인지 물었을 때, 우리는 "그렇다"라고 말했어요. 그리고 만약 그들이 지금 다시 묻는다면, 우리는 "아니다"라고 말하진 않을 겁니다. 우리는 물론, 선생님을 믿지 않는 사람들을 위해서는, 당신이 진짜가 아니라고 말하겠지요. 하지만 선생님을 믿는 사람들에게는 정말 진짜라고 할 겁니다. 우리의 크리스마스 소원은 선생님이 스탠리와 아서 랩찹, 그리고 그들의 부모가 후자의 의견을 취할 거라고 의심하지 않는 것입니다. 진심을 담아, 조지 램찹 부부가, 미국에서.'"

사라의 아버지가 잠시 생각했습니다. "흐으음 . . . 후자의 의견이라고? 아! 정말 믿는다고. 알겠어."

"보셨죠, 아빠?" 사라가 말했습니다. "탐욕이 없어요! 한 사람도—"

"훌륭한 편지야, 사라. 나도 동의한단다." 이제 그 낮은 목소리에는 슬픔이 깃들었습니다. "하지만 사라야, 전부, '납작해졌다는' 이야기로 나를 속일 생각을 한 같은 가족이 보낸 거잖니. 납작하기는!"

램찹 부인이 헉 하고 숨을 내쉬었습니다. "속이다니요? 오, 이런!"

"둥근 것은 둥근 것이지요, 부인." 사라의 아버지가 자신의 고개를 저었습니다. "이 녀석의 형태가 그 사실을 증명하고 있어요."

모든 램찹 가족의 마음이 안에서 내려앉았습니다. 그들의 임무가 실패했다고, 그들은 생각했습니다. 전 세계의 수백만의 아이들에게, 즐거운 휴일이 사라졌고, 아마도 절대 다시 오지 않겠지요.

아서는 특히 기분이 좋지 않았습니다. 그건 내 잘못이야, 라고 그는 자신에게 말했습니다. 자전거 공기 펌프를 생각해내서는 말이야.

스탠리는 가장 기분이 끔찍했습니다. 그가 납작해진 것에 지겨워지지만 않았어도, 아서에게 그를 다시 둥글게 만들어달라고 하지 않았을 겁니다! 만약 증거만 있었더라도—

그리고 그때 그는 무언가를 기억했습니다.

"기다려요!" 그가 외쳤고, 발끝으로 서서 램찹 부인의 귓가에 속삭였습니다.

"뭐 . . . ?" 그녀가 말했습니다. "나는 그럴 수가 없—그 뭐라고? 오! 그래! 나는 잊어버리고 있었어! 잘했다, 스탠리!"

자신의 가방 안을 뒤져서, 그녀는 자신의 지갑을 찾았고, 그 속에서 그녀는 사진 한 장을 꺼냈습니다. 그녀는 그것을 사라의 아버지에게 주었습니다.

"부디 간직해 주세요." 그녀가 말했습니다. "우리는 집에 더 있으니까요."

그 스냅 사진은 큰 게시판이 스탠리 위에 떨어진 다음 날에 램찹 씨가 찍은 것이었습니다. 그것은 꽤 납작한, 그가, 닫힌 문 아래로 미끄러지는 모습을 보여 주었습니다. 단지 그의 상체만이 보였고, 카메라를 향해 미소 짓고 있었습니다. 하체는 여전히 문 뒤에 있었죠.

한참 동안, 사라의 아버지가 그 사진을 살펴보는 동안, 아무도 말하지 않았습니다.

"제가 사과하지요, 램찹 가족." 그가 마침내 말했습니다. "그는 납작하네요. 납작했었죠, 어쨌든. 난 할까 말까 생각했는데—" 그가 한숨 쉬었습니다. "하지만 그 빨간 자동차들, 두 대나 원하다니, 그런—"

"그건 램팝이잖아요!" 아서가 외쳤습니다. "우리가 아니라—"

"그냥 장난친 거야, 녀석!"

사라의 아버지가 벌떡 일어나며, 그의 얼굴에 큰 미소를 지었습니다.

"이봐, 엘프들!" 그가 그의 스피커폰에 대고 외쳤습니다. "선물을 실을 준비를 해! 기운 넘치게 보이라고! 내일은 크리스마스이브라고, 알다시피!"

다음 순간은 정말이지 아주 기뻤습니다.

"고마워요, 고마워요! . . . 만세! . . . 만세! . . . 만세!" 램찹 부부, 그리고 스탠리와 아서와 사라가 외쳤습니다.

사라의 어머니는 모든 사람에게 입을 맞추었습니다. 램찹 부인은 사라의 아버지에게 입 맞추었고, 자신이 한 행동을 깨달았을 때 기절할 뻔했습니다.

그리고는 사라의 아버지는 스탠리에게 문-아래로-미끄러지는 사진에 서명해달라고 부탁했고, 스탠리가 "좋은 일만 가득하기를, S. 램찹"이라고 사진을 가로지르며 적었을 때, 그는 그것을 벽에 꽂았습니다.

"그를 불어서 둥글게 했다고, 응?" 그가 아서에게 말했습니다. "그걸 봤다면 좋았을걸!"

그는 사라에게 돌아섰습니다. "이리 오렴, 내 아가! 내가 몸단장을 하는 동안, 내게 그 순록 이름들을 가르쳐주렴. 그다음에 나는 우리의 손님을 안전하게 집으로 배웅할 거란다!"

6장 집으로 가는 길

엘프들의 무리가 크리스마스 부인과 사라와 함께 작별 인사를 하려고 모였습니다. "고마워요, 램찹!" 그들이 외쳤습니다. "여러분이 와서 정말 다행이에요! . . . 여러분이 오지 않았다고 생각만 해도! . . . 휴! . . . 잘 가요, 잘 가요!"

위대한 썰매 안에서, 사라의 아버지가 고삐를 쥐었습니다. "준비됐나요, 램찹?"

그는 이제 괜찮은 모습을 갖추고 있었는데, 그의 머리카락과 수염은 빗질이 되었고, 선명한 초록색 망토를 입고 모자를 쓰고 있었습니다. 그 유명한 빨간 의상은, 그가 설명하기로는, 선물을 배달하기 위해 따로 마련된 것이라고 했습니다.

"잘 있어요, 모두!" 램찹 부인이 외쳤습니다. "우리는 항상 여러분을 기억할게요!"

"당연하죠!" 스탠리가 소리쳤습니다. "전 절대로 잊지 않을 거예요!"

"하지만 넌 그럴 거란다, 얘야." 크리스마스 부인이 말했습니다. "여러분은 모두 잊게 될 거예요."

"그럴 리가요." 램찹 씨가 미소 지었습니다. "이런 저녁은 사람의 마음에서 잊힐 수가 없어요."

"실은, 아빠가 반드시 그렇게 할 거예요." 사라가 말했습니다. "스노우 시티, 여기에 있는 우리 모두 . . . 우리는 그래야만 해요, 알다시피, 일종의 신비로운 일로 있어야 하지요. 그건 *바보* 같지 않아요? 제 말은, 만약에—"

"사라!" 그녀의 아버지가 말했습니다. "우리는 가야만 한단다."

램찹 가족은 여전히 별들로 환하게 빛나는, 밤하늘을 올려다보았고, 그다음에는 돌아서서 그들 뒤에 있는 작은 빨간 지붕 집, 그리고 눈이 덮인 광장 주위 엘프들의 오두막집의 마지막 모습을 보았습니다.

"우리는 준비됐습니다." 램찹 씨가 말했습니다.

"잘 있어요, 잘 있어요!" 램찹 부인과 스탠리 그리고 아서가 소리쳤습니다.

"잘 가, 잘 가요!" 손을 흔들면서, 엘프들이 외쳤습니다.

여덟 마리의 순록이 그들의 고개를 뒤로 젖히며, 그들의 마구에 달린 종을 딸랑거렸습니다. 한 종이 떨어져 날아갔고, 스탠리가 자신의 손으로 작은 은색 종을 잡았습니다. 갑자기, 전에 그랬듯이, 딸랑거리는 소리가 멈췄고, 온통 조용했고, 옅은 안개가 다시 썰매 주위로 피어올랐습니다.

사라의 아버지의 목소리가 분명하게 울려 퍼졌습니다. "어서, 대셔, 댄서, 프랜서, 빅센! 자, 코멧, 큐피드, 돈더, 그리고 . . . 오, 그 이름이 뭐지?"

"블리츤!" 스탠리가 외쳤습니다.

"고맙구나. 어서 오렴, 블리츤!"

안개가 소용돌이치며, 썰매 위로 덮쳤습니다.

7장 크리스마스

램찹 가족은 모두 다음 날 아침에 그들이 얼마나 깊이, 그리고 얼마나 늦게까지 잠을 잤는지에 대해 말했습니다. 램찹 씨는 서두르며 아침 식사를 했습니다.

"당신 온종일 사무실에 있을 거예요, 조지?" 램찹 부인이 물었습니다. "크리스마스이브이기는 하잖아요, 당신도 알겠지만."

"할 일이 무척 많아요." 램찹 씨가 말했습니다. "유감스럽게도, 난 늦게까지 있어야 할 것 같아요."

하지만 그의 사무실에서는 그를 바쁘게 할 일거리가 거의 없었는데, 왜냐하면 짓궂은 장난꾼이 그가 출근하지 않을 거라고 메시지를 남겼기 때문이었습니다. 그는 정오에는 집에 와서 친구들과 가족과 함께 동네를 돌면서 캐럴을 부르러 다녔습니다.

램찹 부인은 캐럴 부르는 사람들을 안으로 초대해서 코코아를 마시게 했는데, 이는 매우 호평을 받았습니다. 그녀는 시나몬을 넣었는데, 그녀가 설명하기를; 그 생각이 그냥 자신의 머릿속에서 불쑥 떠올랐다고 했습니다. 캐럴을 부르는 사람들은 모두 매우 기뻐했고, 옆집에 사는, 프랭크 스미스는 자신이 전날 밤에 그들의 정원 위에 있는 순록을 보았다고 주장하면서, 모두를, 그중에서도 램찹 가족을 가장 많이 웃게 했습니다.

크리스마스 아침에, 그들은 각자에게 준 그들의 선물과 친척과 친구에서 받은 선물을 풀어 보았습니다. 그리고 깜짝 놀랄 일이 스탠리와 아서에게 일어났습니다. 램찹 씨가 막 TV 뉴스를 틀었습니다.

". . . 그리고 이제 지진이 일어났던, 남미에서 보내온 영상을 보시겠습니다." 아나운서가 말하고 있었습니다. "이곳에 있는 집을 잃은 마을 사람들은 오늘 아침 엄청난 양의 양말, 셔츠, 속옷, 그리고 음식 물품에 대해 감사드렸습니다. 그들은 또 *천 개의 텐트*, 그리고 *천 개의 조리할 수 있는 화로*를 받았습니다!" 화면은 집을 잃은 마을 사람이, 고마워하는 모습을 보여주었습니다. "텐트, 그리고 작은 화로까지." 마을 사람이 말했습니다. "바로 우리가 필요하던 거예요! 누구인지는 몰라도 이 텐트와 화로를 보내준 사람은 축복받을 겁니다! 또 많은 양의 맛있는 견과류가 든 초콜릿 바까지!"

"그를 *나에게* 고마워하고 있어요!" 스탠리가 소리쳤습니다. "전 제 편지에서 텐트를 달라고 했거든요. 하지만 전 그게 일어날지 확신하지 않았어요."

"흠, *제가* 화로에 대해 썼어요." 아서가 말했습니다. "그리고 초콜릿 바에 대해서도. 하지만 그것들은 반드시 견과류가 들어있지 않아도 됐어요."

행복한 우연의 일치야! 라고 램찹 부부는 생각하며, 서로에게 미소를 지었습니다.

많은 이모, 삼촌, 그리고 사촌들과 함께 나눈, 크리스마스 저녁 식사는 칠면조 고기(turkey), 얌(yam), 그리고 세 종류의 파이로 이루어진 엄청난 식사였습니다. 그리고는 모두 공원에 아이스-스케이트를 타러 갔습니다. 잠자리에 들 시간이 되자, 스탠리와 아서는 잠을 잘 준비가 되었습니다.

"괜찮은 휴일이었어." 램찹 씨가 아서에게 이불을 덮어주면서 말했습니다.

"정말 그래요." 램찹 부인이 스탠리에게 이불을 덮어주었습니다. "좋은 꿈꾸렴, 얘들아, 그리고―이게 뭐니?" 그녀는 그의 침대 옆 탁자 위에 있는 무언가를 발견했습니다. "아니, 작은 종이잖아! 은색 종이야!"

"그건 제 주머니 안에 있었어요." 스탠리가 말했습니다. "그게 어디에서 났는지는 모르겠어요."

"예쁘구나. 잘 자렴, 너희 둘." 램찹 부인이 말했고, 불을 껐습니다.

형제는 잠시 어둠 속에서 조용히 누워 있었습니다.

"스탠리 형 . . . ?" 아서가 말했습니다. "오늘은 정말 좋은 휴일이었어, 그렇게 생각하지 않아?"

"굉장히 좋았어." 스탠리가 말했습니

다. "하지만 왜 그럴까? 마치 내가 기억
해야 할 멋진 일이 있지만, 무슨 일인지
떠올릴 수 없는 것 같아."

"나도 그래. 메리 크리스마스, 스탠리
형."

"메리 크리스마스, 아서." 스탠리가 말
했고, 곧 그들은 둘 다 잠이 들었습니
다.

끝

Prologue

1. D At the Post Office, Mail Elves had read the letters, making lists of who wanted what.

2. C In the great workshops—the Doll Room, the Toy Plant, the Game Mill—Gift Elves had filled the orders, taking care as to color and size and style.

3. A In the Wrap Shed the gifts lay ready, wrapped now in gay paper with holly and pine cones, sorted by country, by city or village, by road or lane or street.

4. D "He won't go this year, he says!" The mother sobbed. "He's been so cross lately, but I never—" *"Why? Why* won't he go?" "They've lost faith, don't care anymore, he says!"

5. B *I am a regular boy, except that I got flat,* the letter said. *From an accident. I was going to ask for new clothes, but my mother already bought them. She had to, because of the flatness. So I'm just writing to say don't bother about me. Have a nice holiday.*

Chapter 1

1. C The girl sounded a bit nervous. "Actually, I've never done this before. Let's see . . . Ha, ha, ha! Season's Greetings! Ha, ha, ha!" "'Ha, ha!' to you," said Arthur. "What's so funny?" "Funny?" said the girl. "Oh! 'Ho, ho, ho!' I meant."

2. A "She says her father says he won't come this year, but Sarah thinks he might change his mind if I ask him to. Because I wrote him a letter once that he liked. She wants me to go with her to Snow City."

3. D "It's a pillowcase." Arthur blushed. "My stocking wouldn't do. I have very small feet." "Pooh!" Sarah laughed. "You wanted extra gifts, so—"

4. B "Hello, George," the caller said. "This is your neighbor, Frank Smith. I know it's late, but I must congratulate you on your Christmas lawn display! Best—" "Lawn?" said Mr. Lambchop. "Display?" "The sleigh! And those lifelike *reindeer!* What makes them move about like that? Batteries, I suppose?"

5. A Mrs. Lambchop thought they should wait until Frank Smith had gone to bed. "Imagine the gossip," she said, "were he to see our reindeer fly away."

Chapter 2

1. B The Lambchops, sitting on little benches that made the big sleigh resemble a roofless bus, could scarcely contain their excitement.

2. D Sarah cleared her throat. "Fasten your seat belts, please! We are about to depart for Snow City. My name is Sarah—I guess you know that—and I'll be glad to answer any questions you may have. Please do not move about without permission of the Sleigh Master—that's me, at least right now—and obey whatever instructions may—"

3. C The Lambchops fastened their seat belts, and Sarah took up the reins. "Ready, One? Ready, Two, Three—" "Just *numbers*?" cried Mrs. Lambchop. "Why, we know such lovely reindeer names! Dasher, Dancer, Prancer, Vixen—"

4. C The reindeer pawed the ground, jingling their harness bells. "Now!" said Sarah. The jingling stopped suddenly, and a great silence fell. Now a silver mist rose, swirling, about the sleigh.

5. A "What is this, Sarah?" Mrs. Lambchop called. "Are we not to proceed to Snow City?" Sarah's voice came cheerfully through the mist. "We have proceeded. We're there!"

Chapter 3

1. B The elves seemed much like ordinary men and women, except that they had pointy ears, very wrinkled faces, and were only about half as tall as Arthur. All wore leather breeches or skirts with wide pockets from which tools and needles stuck out.

2. D "Miss Sarah!" came a voice. "Is it true? He won't go this year?" Sarah hesitated. "Well, sort of . . . But perhaps the Lambchops here . . . Be patient. Go home, please!" The elves straggled off toward their cottages, grumbling. "Not going?" . . . "Hah! After all our work?"

3. A "Sarah! Are you all right? Going off like that! Though we did find your note."

4. B Mrs. Christmas knocked on a door. "Visitors, dear! From America." "Send 'em back!" said a deep voice. "Sir?" Mr. Lambchop tried to sound cheerful. "A few minutes, perhaps? ''Tis the season to be jolly,' eh? We—" "Bah!" said the voice. "Go home!"

5. C Sarah stepped forward. "Poppa? Can you hear me, Poppa?" "I hear you, all right!" said the deep voice. "Took the Great Sleigh without permission, didn't you? Rascal!"

Chapter 4

1. D Except for a large TV in one corner and a speaker-box on the desk, the room was much like Mr. Lambchop's study at home. There were bookshelves and comfortable chairs. Framed letters, one of them Stanley's, hung behind the desk, along with photographs of Mrs. Christmas, Sarah, and elves and reindeer, singly and in groups.

2. A Sarah's father was large and stout, but otherwise not what they had expected. He wore a blue zip jacket with "N. Pole Athletic Club" lettered across it, and sat with his feet, in fuzzy brown slippers, up on the desk. His long white hair and beard were in need of trimming, and the beard had crumbs in it. On the desk, along with his feet, were a plate of cookies, a bowl of potato chips, and a bottle of strawberry soda with a straw in it.

3. C Mr. Lambchop cleared his throat. "I understand, Mr.—No, that can't be right. What *is* the proper form of address?" "Depends where you're from. 'Santa' is the American way. But I'm known also as Father Christmas, *Père Noel, Babbo Natale, Julenisse* . . . Little country, way off somewhere, they call me 'The Great Hugga Wagoo.'"

4. C The big TV in the corner clicked on, and he switched from channel to channel. The first channel showed battleships firing flaming missiles; the second, airplanes dropping bombs; the third, cars crashing other cars. Then came buildings burning, people begging for food, people hitting each other, people firing pistols at policemen. The last channel showed a game show, men and women in chicken costumes grabbing for prizes in a pool of mud. Sarah's father switched off the TV. "Peace on Earth? Goodwill toward men? Been wasting my time, it seems!"

5. B "You misjudge us, sir," he said. "There is indeed much violence in the world, and selfishness. But not everyone—we Lambchops, for example—"

Chapter 5

1. A "'Dear Santa, My parents say I can't have a real car until I'm grown up. I want one now. A big red one. Make that two cars, both red.' Hah! Hear that? Shameful!" Mrs. Lambchop shook her head. "I should be interested," she said, "to learn who wrote that letter?" "It is signed—hmmmm . . . Frederic. Frederic Lampop." Stanley laughed. "Our name's not 'Lampop!' And we don't even know any Frederics!" "Mistakes *do* happen, you know! I get *millions* of letters!"

2. B "'Dear Santa,' he read. 'I hope you are fine. I need lots of gifts this year. Shoes and socks and shirts and pants and underwear. And big tents. At least a hundred of each would be nice—' A hundred! *There's* greediness!" "It does seem a bit much, Stanley," said Mr. Lambchop. "And why tents, for goodness sake?" "You'll see," said Stanley. Sarah's father read on. " '. . . of each would be nice. But not delivered to my house. It was on TV about a terrible earthquake in South America where all the houses fell down, and people lost all their clothes and don't have anywhere to live. Please take everything to where the earthquake was.'"

3. C "'Dear Sir: Perhaps you expect letters from children only, since as people grow older they often begin to doubt that you truly exist. But when our two sons were very small, and asked if you were real, we said "yes." And if they were to ask again now, we would not say "no." We would say that you are not real, of course, for those who do not believe in you, but very real indeed for those who *do*. Our Christmas wish is that you will never have cause to doubt that Stanley and Arthur Lambchop, and their parents, take the latter position.'"

4. D "Fine letters, Sarah. I agree." There was sadness in the deep voice now. "But all, Sarah, from the same family that thought to deceive me with that 'flatness' story. Flat indeed!" Mrs. Lambchop gasped. "Deceive? Oh, no!" "Round is round, madam." Sarah's father shook his head. "The lad's shape speaks for itself."

5. B Then Sarah's father asked Stanley to autograph the sliding-under-the-door picture, and when Stanley had written "All best wishes, S. Lambchop" across the picture, he pinned it to the wall.

Chapter 6

1. C A crowd of elves had gathered with Mrs. Christmas and Sarah to say good-bye. "Bless you, Lambchops!" they called. "Thank goodness you came! . . . Think if you hadn't! . . . Whew! . . . Farewell, farewell!"

2. A He made a fine appearance now, his hair and beard combed, and wearing a smart green cloak and cap. The famous red suit, he had explained, was reserved for delivering gifts.

3. C "Good-bye, everyone!" called Mrs. Lambchop. "We will remember you always!" "You bet!" cried Stanley. "I'll *never* forget!"

4. A "Snow City, all of us here . . . We're supposed to be, you know, sort of a mystery."

5. B The eight reindeer tossed their heads, jingling their harness bells. One bell flew off, and Stanley caught the little silver cup in his hand.

Chapter 7

1. B Mrs. Lambchop had the carolers in for hot chocolate, which was greatly admired. She had added cinnamon, she explained; the idea had just popped into her head.

2. C The carolers were all very jolly, and Frank Smith, who lived next door, made everyone laugh, the Lambchops hardest of all, by claiming he had seen reindeer on their lawn the night before.

3. C "The tents, and the little stoves," the villager said. "Just what we need! Bless whoever sends these tents and stoves! Also the many tasty chocolate bars with nuts!" "He's blessing *me!*" cried Stanley. "I asked for tents in my letter. But I wasn't sure it would work." "Well, I wrote about stoves." Arthur said. "*And* chocolate bars. But they didn't have to have nuts." Happy coincidences! thought Mr. and Mrs. Lambchop, smiling at each other.

4. B Mrs. Lambchop tucked in Stanley. "Pleasant dreams, boys, and—What's this?" She had found something on the table by his bed. "Why, it's a little bell! A silver bell!" "It was in my pocket," Stanley said. "I don't know what it's from."

5. A "Stanley . . . ?" Arthur said. "It was a nice holiday, don't you think?" "*Extra* nice," said Stanley. "But why? It's as if I have something wonderful to remember, but can't think what." "Me too. Merry Christmas, Stanley."

스탠리의 크리스마스 모험
(Stanley's Christmas Adventure)

1판 1쇄   2017년 9월 4일
2판 1쇄   2024년 10월 21일

지은이   Jeff Brown
기획   이수영
책임편집   김보경 정소이
콘텐츠제작및감수   롱테일 교육 연구소
저작권   명채린
마케팅   두잉글 사업 본부

펴낸이   이수영
펴낸곳   롱테일북스
출판등록   제2015-000191호
주소   04033 서울특별시 마포구 양화로 113, 3층(서교동, 순흥빌딩)
전자메일   help@ltinc.net

ISBN 979-11-91343-67-0 14740